Author's Profile

Paul Baweja was born in Sydney, the Commonwealth of Australia. Paul Baweja was educated at LaSalle Catholic College (Sydney, New South Wales), the college of the former Australian Prime Minister, the Right Honourable Paul John Keating of the Commonwealth of Australia (r. 1991–1996). Paul Baweja earned the Bachelor of Commerce from Macquarie University in 2012, and he attained the Graduate Diploma of Chartered Accounting from the Institute of Chartered Accountants Australia in 2014. Paul is the recipient of numerous academic awards, including the prestigious 'Golden Key International Honour Society' Award.

In addition, Paul attended the Macquarie Business School (Macquarie University) to obtain the Master of Business Administration in 2016. Paul further completed research-based postgraduate study at the Australian National University, graduating with the Master of Diplomacy (Advanced) in 2018.

Paul Baweja is an Australian author and writer. Baweja has been studying philosophy in excess of 20 years, he demonstrates an ardent passion for philosophical inquiry and discourse, which over the course of the former eight years and nine months, has led him to write *A Philosophical Treatise of Reality* (2021), a half-a-million-word four volume treatise.

A Philosophical TREATISE *of* REALITY

— VOLUME III OF IV —

FIRST EDITION

PAUL BAWEJA

MMXXI

First published in Melbourne,
the Commonwealth of Australia, 2021

Published by Paul Baweja

APTOR2021_enquiries@protonmail.com

Copyright © Paul Baweja, 2021

First Edition 2021 (Hardcover Book)

The moral right of the author has been asserted.

All rights reserved. No part of this book may be reproduced in any form or by any electronic or mechanical means, including, but not limited to, information storage and retrieval systems, without permission in writing from the author, except as permitted by copyright law.

The author has no responsibility for the persistence or accuracy of URL's for external or third-party internet websites referred to in this publication and does not guarantee that any content on such websites is, or will remain, accurate or available.

A Philosophical Treatise of Reality is written and published in accordance with the tenets of International Law. Specifically, pursuant to Article 19 of *The Universal Declaration of Human Rights (1948)* which explicitly states that: 'Everyone has the right to freedom of opinion and expression; this right includes freedom to hold opinions without interference and to seek, receive and impart information and ideas through any media and regardless of frontiers'.

Reasonable endeavours have been made to contact and acknowledge copyright holders of material reproduced in this treatise. I would be pleased to rectify any omissions in subsequent editions should they be drawn to my attention.

 A catalogue record for this book is available from the National Library of Australia

ISBN: 978 0 6489818 1 7 (Volume I of IV—Hardcover Book)
ISBN: 978 0 6489818 2 4 (Volume II of IV—Hardcover Book)
ISBN: 978 0 6489818 3 1 (Volume III of IV—Hardcover Book)
ISBN: 978 0 6489818 4 8 (Volume IV of IV—Hardcover Book)

Editing and proofreading by True Editors (London)
Design and typesetting by Blue Wren Books (Melbourne)
Printed by Ingram Spark

Treatise Dedication

I dedicate this philosophical treatise to the memory of the Right Honourable Nelson Mandela (1918–2013). Mandela was a South African revolutionary political leader, whose profound life story and struggle for equality is an inspiration to all the people of the world.

Author's Acknowledgements

National Museum of Australia (Australia)
State Library of Queensland (Australia)
State Library of New South Wales (Australia)
National Library of Australia (Australia)
Museums Victoria (Australia)
Australian War Memorial (Australia)
State Library of Western Australia (Australia)
National Archives of Australia (Australia)
Australian Human Rights Commission (Australia)
Australian Bureau of Statistics (Australia)
National Native Title Tribunal (Australia)
Library and Archives Canada (Canada)
Statistics Canada (Canada)
European Space Agency (France)
Organisation for Economic Co-operation and Development (France)
Federal Archives (Germany)
UN Dept. of Economic & Social Affairs (New York, International Territory)
International Court of Justice (the Hague, Netherlands)
Archives New Zealand (New Zealand)
New Zealand Parliamentary Library (New Zealand)
New Zealand Ministry for Culture and Heritage (New Zealand)
International Committee of the Red Cross (Geneva, Switzerland)
Middle Temple Library (United Kingdom)
Royal Geographical Society (United Kingdom)
British Library (United Kingdom)
Wellcome Library (United Kingdom)
Imperial War Museum (United Kingdom)
National Archives (United Kingdom)
Natural History Museum (United Kingdom)
Historic England Archive (United Kingdom)
Royal Observatory Edinburgh (Scotland, United Kingdom)

Science and Society Picture Library (United Kingdom)
Science Photo Library (United Kingdom)
King's College London Archives (United Kingdom)
Ministry of Information (United Kingdom)
Financial Times (United Kingdom)
Jimmy Carter Presidential Library and Museum (United States)
Franklin Roosevelt Library (United States)
New York Public Library (United States)
New York Historical Society (United States)
American Philosophical Society (United States)
Art Institute of Chicago (United States)
National Archives and Records Administration (United States)
Library of Congress (United States)
Granger Historical Picture Archive (United States)
National Geographic Magazine Archive (United States)
American Psychological Association (United States)
National Aeronautics and Space Administration (United States)
Time Magazine Archive (United States)
National Science Foundation (United States)
National Museum of American History (United States)
United States Holocaust Memorial Museum (United States)
Virginia Museum of Fine Arts (United States)
Smithsonian Museum of American Art (United States)
United States Department of Defence (United States)
United States Department of State (United States)
Richard Nixon Presidential Library and Museum (United States)
Harry S. Truman Presidential Library and Museum (United States)

Contents

Timeline	xi
List of Figures	xv
List of Abbreviations	xxi
Preface	xxix

VOLUME I
Introduction	1
1. Conventional Reality: *Stanzas 1–299*	9
2. Ultimate Reality: *Stanzas 300–567*	397

VOLUME II
3. Classical Philosophy: *Stanzas 568–897*	619
4. Morality, Ethics, and Theology: *Stanzas 898–958*	747

VOLUME III
5. Medicine: *Stanzas 959–970*	831
6. History and Jurisprudence: *Stanzas 971–1,000*	855

VOLUME IV
7. Politics, Diplomacy, and War: *Stanzas 1,001–1,038*	1015
8. Commerce and Economics: *Stanzas 1,039–1,094*	1297
Conclusion	1491
Bibliography	1505
Foreign Language to English Translation of Key Words	1647
Glossary	1659
Index	1811

Timeline

ca. 4 BC	The Birth of Jesus Christ
ca. 30 AD	The Crucifixion of Jesus Christ
66–73	The First Jewish-Roman War
70	The Siege of Jerusalem
115–117	The Kitos War
132–135	The Bar Kokhba Revolt (also known as the Second Jewish Revolt)
206	The Silk Road is established by China's Han Dynasty
220	The Collapse of the Han Dynasty
319–467	The Golden Age of India
410	The Sack of Rome
537–538	The Siege of Rome
535–554	The Gothic War
541–542	The Plague of Justinian
550	The Fall of the Gupta Empire (India)
570	The Birth of Prophet Muhammad (Peace be upon Him)
604	Saint Paul's Cathedral is established in London
634–638	The Muslim conquest of the Levant
793	The Vikings sack the Holy Island of Lindisfarne
871–899	Alfred the Great rules as the King of Wessex
1054	The Great Schism (also known as The East-West Schism)
1066	The Battle of Hastings
1096–1099	The First Crusade
1147–1149	The Second Crusade
1189–1192	The Third Crusade
1202–1204	The Fourth Crusade
1215	The Magna Carter is issued by His Majesty King John of England
1215	The birth of the English Parliament
1217–1221	The Fifth Crusade
1228–1229	The Sixth Crusade

1248–1254	The Seventh Crusade
1270	The Eighth Crusade
1271–1272	The Ninth Crusade (also known as Lord Edward's Crusade)
1315–1317	The Great Famine
1337–1453	The Hundred Years' War
1346–1352	The Black Death
1350	The Renaissance begins in Florence, Italy
1378–1417	The Western Schism (also known as The Papal Schism)
1453	Fall of Constantinople
1455–1485	The Wars of the Roses
1492	Christopher Columbus discovers America
1517	Martin Luther posts Ninety-Five Theses to the door of the Castle Church in Wittenberg, Germany
1529	The Siege of Vienna
1600	The British East India Company was incorporated
1607	First permanent English settlement in North America – Jamestown, Virginia
1618–1648	The Thirty Years' War
1642–1651	The English Civil War
1665–1666	The Great Plague of London
1683	The Siege of Vienna
1688–1689	The Glorious Revolution in England
1707	The Union of England and Scotland
1757	The Battle of Plassey
1775	The Battles of Lexington and Concord
1776	U.S. Declaration of Independence
1781	The Siege of Yorktown
1788	The founding of Australia by Captain Arthur Phillip
1789–1799	The French Revolution
1803–1815	The Napoleonic Wars
1815	The Battle of Waterloo
1840–1842	The First Opium War
1856–1860	The Second Opium War
1857–1859	The Sepoy Mutiny
1861–1865	The American Civil War
1863	Founding of the International Committee of the Red Cross (formerly known as the International Committee for Relief to the Wounded)
1865	The Assassination of U.S. President Abraham Lincoln
1868–1889	The Meiji Restoration (Japan)

TIMELINE

1893	New Zealand grants women the right to vote in parliamentary elections
1895–1898	Cuban War of Independence
1898	The Spanish-American War
1899	The First Hague Convention
1899–1901	The Boxer Rebellion
1901	The establishment of the Commonwealth of Australia
1907	The Second Hague Convention
1912	Republic of China established with Sun Yat-sen as the Provisional President
1914–1918	World War I
1917	The Russian Revolution
1918–1920	The Spanish Flu Pandemic
1920	Formation of the League of Nations
1933	Adolf Hitler becomes the Chancellor of Germany
1937–1945	Japan's War against China
1939–1945	World War II
1941	Japan surprise attack on Pearl Harbour
1942	The Fall of Singapore
1944	The Normandy Landings (Operation Overlord)
1945	U.S. atomic bombings of Hiroshima and Nagasaki
1945	Formation of the United Nations
1947	India gains its Independence from British colonial rule
1948	The Assassination of Mahatma Gandhi
1949	Founding of the People's Republic of China
1950–1953	The Korean War
1955–1975	The Vietnam War
1957	Soviet Union's launch of Sputnik 1
1962	The Cuban Missile Crisis
1968	The Assassination of Martin Luther King, Jr.
1978	U.S. President Carter hosts peace talks at Camp David between Egyptian President Sadat and Israeli Prime Minister Begin
1979	Establishment of diplomatic relations between United States and the People's Republic of China
1989	Tim Berners-Lee invented the World Wide Web (WWW)
1989	Fall of the Berlin Wall
1990	German Reunification
1994	Nelson Mandela becomes the President of South Africa
2001	September 11, 2001 Terrorist Attacks
2001	China joins the World Trade Organisation (WTO)
2019	SARS-CoV-2 Pandemic

List of Figures

VOLUME I

1. Charles Darwin, the British naturalist. — 29
2. The Garden of Eden with the Fall of Man. — 85
3. The Creation of Adam. — 91
4. The Marxist revolutionary leader Che Guevara. — 183
5. The English playwright and poet William Shakespeare. — 185
6. The Biblical story of Cain slaying Abel. — 206
7. Lizzie van Zyl, a South African child inmate of the British concentration camps who died from Typhoid fever, but was starved to death by the British, as her father, Hermanus Egbert Pieter Van Zyl fought against the British in the Second Anglo-Boer War (1899–1902). — 226
8. The Vietnamese Buddhist monk *Thích Quảng Đức*'s self-immolation in Vietnam, 1963. — 227
9. The French philosopher and mathematician René Descartes. — 260
10. Sir William Henry Perkin's original stoppered bottle of mauveine dye. — 284
11. Photograph of the original culture plate of the fungus Penicillium notatum discovered by Sir Alexander Fleming at St. Mary's Hospital in London, 1928. — 285
12. The Italian fascist dictator Benito Mussolini gives a speech in 1935. — 290
13. The corpse of Italian fascist leader Benito Mussolini hangs by his feet at a petrol station in Milan (third from the left), after his execution by Partisans at Mezzegra, 1945. — 292
14. The British Empire in 1897. — 299
15. The South African anti-apartheid revolutionary and political leader Nelson Mandela. — 340
16. Degree of Ossification of a Five-Month-Old Fetus. — 357
17. Foetus in amniotic sac at 16 weeks (I of II). — 362
18. Foetus in amniotic sac at 16 weeks (II of II). — 363

19. A woman is arrested for defying Chicago's edict that bans bathing suits on beaches, 1922. 391
20. Mr. Buchanan from the West Palm Beach Police Force, measures the bathing suit of Betty Fringle on Palm Beach, Florida in 1925. 392
21. A group of models celebrate during a world record attempt for the biggest swimsuit photo shoot at Bondi Beach on September 26, 2007 in Sydney, Australia. 393
22. Biafra, Nto Edino rest centre. Distribution of food to malnourished children. 415
23. The German-born theoretical physicist Albert Einstein. 427
24. The Periodic Classification of the Elements. 437
25. The German philosopher Immanuel Kant. 459
26. The Italian artist, engineer, scientist, and inventor Leonardo da Vinci. 519
27. The Austrian Catholic monk and botanist Gregor Mendel. 520
28. The French chemist and microbiologist Louis Pasteur. 521
29. The Serbian-American engineer, inventor, and physicist Nikola Tesla. 522
30. The English natural philosopher and mathematician Sir Isaac Newton. 535
31. The Polish Astronomer and mathematician Nicolaus Copernicus. 544
32. The Italian astronomer and natural philosopher Galileo Galilei. 545
33. The German theoretical physicist Max Planck. 550

VOLUME II

34. Speech by Adolf Hitler at the Kroll Opera House in Berlin, 1941. 634
35. The English actress and model Elizabeth Hurley reclines on a bed in black lace lingerie, London, 1992. 757
36. The martyrdom of Ridley and Latimer, 1555. 767
37. The Archbishop of Canterbury Cranmer is burnt alive in 1556. 768
38. The Crucifixion of Jesus Christ. 770
39. The German Professor of Theology and Priest Martin Luther. 772

VOLUME III

40. Human head, MRI, and 3D CT scans. 848
41. Dolly was the world's first cloned sheep. 851
42. Snuppy, right, the first cloned Afghan hound, next to his genetic father. 851

LIST OF FIGURES

43. John Badby being burned in a barrel at St. Bartholomew's in Smithfield for heresy as a Lollard in 1410. — 864
44. The English Lollard Leader Sir John Oldcastle being burned in St. Giles in the Fields for insurrection and Lollard heresy in 1417. — 864
45. The 16th U.S. President Abraham Lincoln. — 867
46. The Reverend Dr. Martin Luther King, Jr. — 872
47. Women's Suffrage Petition to the New Zealand Parliament. — 873
48. Chinese Boxer Rebellions executed upon their defeat by foreign belligerent nation-states. — 884
49. Malnourished Russian children during the Russian famine, 1921–1923. — 886
50. British educated Indian lawyer and anti-colonial nationalist Mahatma Gandhi. — 890
51. The foundation of the modern British Commonwealth of Australia by Captain Arthur Phillip at Sydney Cove, 1788. — 912
52. Rosie the Riveter. — 928
53. The British scientist Rosalind Elsie Franklin. — 934
54. Watson and Crick discover the structure of DNA. — 935
55. The White Australia National Song, 1910. — 955
56. A Federation-era flag or bunting. — 956
57. The German astronomer and mathematician Johannes Kepler. — 982
58. The Dutch philosopher Baruch Spinoza. — 983
59. The Danish astronomer and mathematician Tycho Brahe. — 984

VOLUME IV

60. The signing of the Declaration of Independence on July 4, 1776 in Philadelphia. — 1065
61. The Surrender of Cornwallis at Yorktown, 1781 AD. — 1067
62. George Washington presiding at the Constitutional Convention at Philadelphia in 1787. — 1067
63. Founding Father and the first President of the United States, George Washington. — 1069
64. The French military and political leader Napoleon Bonaparte. — 1076
65. A Hundred Years Peace. The Signature of the Treaty of Ghent between Great Britain and the United States of America, Dec. 24th 1814, ca. 1915. — 1077
66. An escaped slave named Gordon, also known as 'Whipped Peter', exposes his scarred back at a medical examination in Baton Rouge, Louisiana, the United States. — 1080

67. The execution of the thirty-eight Sioux Indians at Mankato, Minnesota, December 26, 1862. — 1088
68. Burial of the dead after the massacre of Wounded Knee. U.S. Soldiers putting Indians in a common grave. — 1098
69. Operation Castle Bravo, 1956. — 1109
70. The mushroom cloud of the U.S. atomic bombing of *Nagasaki*, Japan on 9 August 1945. — 1121
71. The U.S. Marines raise the U.S. flag at *Mount Suribachi, Iwo Jima*, Japan 1945. — 1122
72. The U.S. General Douglas MacArthur signs the formal Japanese surrender instrument on board the U.S.S. *Missouri* in Tokyo Bay on 2 September 1945. — 1125
73. The Japanese surprise attack on Pearl Harbour, 1941. — 1126
74. Three U.S. battleships are hit from the air during the Japanese surprise military attack on Pearl Harbour on 7 December 1941. The three battleships from left to right are: the U.S.S. *West Virginia*, the U.S.S. *Tennessee*, and the U.S.S. *Arizona*. — 1126
75. The U.S. Air Force fighter jets fly over Imperial Japan's airspace upon its acceptance of the surrender instrument in Tokyo Bay. — 1129
76. U.S. President Harry S. Truman inspects the famed 442nd Regimental Combat Team. — 1139
77. The Sharpeville Massacre in South Africa on 21 March 1960. — 1148
78. Mr. Churchill with the Commonwealth Prime Ministers, 1944. — 1149
79. Vietnamese children flee from their homes in the South Vietnamese village of *Trang Bang* after U.S. napalm bombing. — 1154
80. The My Lai Massacre, the mass murder of 347 to 504 unarmed citizens of the Republic of Vietnam (South Vietnam), almost entirely civilians and the majority of them women and children, perpetrated by the U.S.' Army Forces on March 16, 1968. — 1154
81. The September 11, 2001 Terror Attack. — 1158
82. Manhattan: The Statue of Liberty and Liberty Island, 1898. — 1164
83. Chamberlain, Mussolini, and Hitler at the Munich Conference, Germany, 29 September 1938; the gentleman between Hitler and Chamberlain was Hitler's interpreter; Paul Otto Gustav Schmidt. — 1181
84. Chamberlain arrives at Heston Airport with the Munich Agreement (1938) signed by Hitler. — 1182
85. The Battle of Britain 1940. — 1211
86. The British Prime Minister, the Right Honourable Sir Winston Leonard Spencer Churchill. — 1212

LIST OF FIGURES

87.	The remains of St Thomas's Church viewed from the east following bomb damage (Birmingham, 1941).	1214
88.	Execution of Poles by the Germans, Poland, 1939–1945 War.	1216
89.	The U.S. President Carter, the Egyptian President Sadat, and the Israeli Prime Minister Begin celebrate the signing of the 'Treaty of Peace Between the Arab Republic of Egypt and the State of Israel'.	1226
90.	The Quebec Conference, Canada, August 1943.	1263
91.	Pamphlet—'Twenty Million Australians in Our Time!', the Honourable Arthur Calwell, Australian Federal Minister for Immigration, 8 September 1949.	1267
92.	Pamphlet—'I Stand By White Australia', the Honourable Arthur Calwell, Australian Federal Minister for Immigration, 24 October 1949.	1268
93.	*Führer* Adolf Hitler ascends the steps to the speaker's podium during the 1934 harvest festival at *Buckenburg*, Germany.	1277
94.	The Putilov Strike on 23 February 1917 by Russian workers in Petrograd.	1286
95.	East and West Germans celebrate the lifting of travel restrictions on East Germans on a section of the Berlin Wall in front of the Brandenburg Gate, November 1989.	1291
96.	The German philosopher, economist, historian, and sociologist Karl Marx.	1308
97.	The Scottish economist and philosopher Adam Smith.	1359
98.	The English economist John Maynard Keynes.	1402

List of Abbreviations

ABS	Australian Bureau of Statistics
ACT	Australian Capital Territory (Australia)
AD	Anno Domini
AEC	Australian Electoral Commission
AHRC	Australian Human Rights Commission
AI	Amnesty International
AIATSIS	Australian Institute of Aboriginal and Torres Strait Islander Studies
AIDS	Acquired Immunodeficiency Syndrome
ALJR	Australian Law Journal Reports
ALR	American Law Reports
ALR	Australian Law Reports
AML	Anti-Money Laundering
ANC	African National Congress
ANS	Autonomic Nervous System
ANZUS	Australia, New Zealand, and the United States Security Treaty
APA	American Psychological Association
ASEAN	Association of Southeast Asian Nations
ATIC	Australian Trade and Investment Commission
ATM	Automated Teller Machine
AU	Australia
AUD	Australian Dollar
AURA	Association of Universities for Research in Astronomy
AUS	Australia
AUSTRAC	Australian Transaction Reports and Analysis Centre
AWM	Australian War Memorial
BATNA	Best Alternative To Negotiated Outcome
BBB	Blood-Brain Barrier
BC	Before Christ
BIOT	British Indian Ocean Territory
BJP	Bharatiya Janata Party

BMJ	British Medical Journal
BOP	Balance of Payments
BPM	Beats Per Minute
BRIC	Brazil, Russia, India, and China
CAD	Current Account Deficit
CAN	Canada
CAP	Common Agricultural Policy
CBA	Commonwealth Bank of Australia
CCP	Chinese Communist Party
CEO	Chief Executive Officer
CERD	Convention on the Elimination of Racial Discrimination
CERN	European Organisation for Nuclear Research
CES	Common Economic Space
CFO	Chief Financial Officer
CIA	Central Intelligence Agency
CIS	Commonwealth of Independent States
CLR	Commonwealth Law Reports
CMO	Chief Medical Officer
CNS	Central Nervous System
CoE	Council of Europe
CPSU	Communist Party of the Soviet Union
CSR	Corporate Social Responsibility
CTH	Commonwealth
CWC	Chemical Weapons Convention
DMZ	De-Militarised Zone
DNA	Deoxyribonucleic Acid
D.P.R.K.	Democratic People's Republic of Korea
DSM	Dispute Settlement Mechanism
EBRD	European Bank for Reconstruction and Development
ECCC	Extraordinary Chambers in the Courts of Cambodia
ECHR	European Convention on Human Rights
ECJ	European Court of Justice
EEC	European Economic Community
EFTA	European Free Trade Association
EOI	Export Oriented Industrialisation
ESA	European Space Agency
EU	European Union
FAO	Food and Agriculture Organisation
FDI	Foreign Direct Investment
FOL	First Order Logic

LIST OF ABBREVIATIONS

FTA	Free Trade Agreement
G5	Group of 5 (Britain, France, Germany, Japan, and the United States)
G7	Group of 7 (G5, plus Canada and Italy)
G8	Group of 8 (G5, plus Canada, Italy, and Russia)
G20	Group of 20
G77	United Nations General Assembly Group of 77
GATS	General Agreement on Trade in Services
GATT	General Agreement on Tariffs and Trade
GCC	Gulf Cooperation Council
GDP	Gross Domestic Product
GFC	Global Financial Crisis
GNP	Gross National Product
GWOT	Global War on Terror
HCA	High Court of Australia
HCCH	Hague Conference on Private International Law
HGP	Human Genome Project
HIC	High Income Countries
HIV	Human Immunodeficiency Virus
HK	Hong Kong
HOPOS	International Society for the History of Philosophy of Science
HRE	Holy Roman Empire
HRLC	Human Rights Law Centre
HRW	Human Rights Watch
HSBC	Hongkong and Shanghai Banking Corporation
IAEA	International Atomic Energy Agency
IAI	Israel Aerospace Industries
IBM	International Business Machines Corporation
IBRD	International Bank for Reconstruction and Development
ICC	International Criminal Court
ICCPR	International Covenant on Civil and Political Rights
ICESCR	International Covenant on Economic, Social, and Cultural Rights
ICJ	International Court of Justice
ICRC	International Committee of the Red Cross
ICT	Information and Communications Technology
ICTB	International Criminal Tribunal of Bangladesh
ICTR	International Criminal Tribunal for Rwanda
ICTY	International Criminal Tribunal for the former Yugoslavia
ICWM	International Committee for Weights and Measures

IDWIP	International Day of the World's Indigenous Peoples
IEA	International Energy Agency
IFC	International Finance Corporation
IGO	Inter-Governmental Organisation
IJA	Imperial Japanese Army
ILO	International Labour Organisation
IMF	International Monetary Fund
IMT	International Monetary Theory
IMTN	International Military Tribunal at Nuremberg
IO	International Organisation
IOLM	International Organisation of Legal Metrology
IOS	International Organisation for Standardisation
IPCC	Intergovernmental Panel on Climate Change
IPCL	International Peace Cooperation Law
IRGC	Islamic Revolutionary Guard Corps
ISIS	Islamic State of Iraq and Syria
ITUC	International Trade Union Confederation
IUCN	International Union for Conservation of Nature
IUPAC	International Union of Pure and Applied Chemistry
IVF	In Vitro Fertilisation
IWM	Imperial War Museum
JPY	Japanese Yen
JSDF	Japanese Self Defence Forces
LAC	Library and Archives Canada
LDC	Least Developed Countries
LED	Light-Emitting Diode
LHC	Large Hadron Collider
LNG	Liquefied Natural Gas
LoC	Library of Congress
LTI	Long Term Incentives
MAD	Mutually Assured Destruction
MI6	Secret Intelligence Service
MMT	Modern Monetary Theory
MoU	Memorandum of Understanding
MPC	Marginal Propensity to Consume
MPS	Marginal Propensity to Save
NAA	National Archives of Australia
NAFTA	North American Free Trade Agreement
NAM	Non-Aligned Movement
NARA	National Archives and Records Administration

LIST OF ABBREVIATIONS

NASA	National Aeronautics and Space Administration
NATO	North Atlantic Treaty Organisation
NAZI	National Socialist German Workers' Party
NFP	Not For Profit
NGO	Non-Government Organisation
NIAS	National Institute of Advanced Studies
NIH	National Institutes of Health
NJ	New Jersey (United States)
NLA	National Library of Australia
NMA	National Museum of Australia
NMAH	National Museum of American History
NNTT	National Native Title Tribunal
NPT	Non-Proliferation Treaty
NSW	New South Wales (Australia)
NT	Northern Territory (Australia)
NTA	Native Title Act 1993 (Cth)
NTER	Northern Territory Emergency Response
NWR	Nordic Wittgenstein Review
NYC	New York City (United States)
NZ	New Zealand
OAS	Organisation of American States
OAU	Organisation of African Unity
OECD	Organisation for Economic Co-operation and Development
OPCW	Organisation for the Prohibition of Chemical Weapons
OPEC	Organisation of the Petroleum Exporting Countries
P5	UN Security Council Permanent Five Members
PCA	Permanent Court of Arbitration (the Hague)
PFC	Private First Class
pH	Potential of Hydrogen
PLO	Palestine Liberation Organisation
POW	Prisoner of War
PPP	Purchasing Power Parity
PRC	People's Republic of China
QE	Quantitative Easing
QLD	Queensland (Australia)
R&D	Research and Development
R2P	Responsibility to Protect
RCEP	Regional Comprehensive Economic Partnership
RNA	Ribonucleic Acid
ROC	Republic of China

SA	South Australia (Australia)
S&P	Standard & Poor's Global Ratings
SAR	Special Administrative Region
SARS	Severe Acute Respiratory Syndrome
SCO	Shanghai Cooperation Organisation
SEAL	Sea, Air, and Land Forces
SEZ	Special Economic Zone
SFRY	Socialist Federal Republic of Yugoslavia
SI	International System of Units
SLNSW	State Library of New South Wales
SMBH	Super-Massive Black Hole
SMT	Standard Model of Particle Physics Theory
SOL	Second Order Logic
SPSS	Statistical Package for the Social Sciences
STI	Short Term Incentives
STSCI	Space Telescope Science Institute
ToR	Terms of Reference
TPP	Trans-Pacific Partnership
TRIPS	Trade-Related Aspects of Intellectual Property Rights
U.A.E.	United Arab Emirates
UDHR	Universal Declaration of Human Rights
U.K.	United Kingdom of Great Britain and Northern Ireland
UKOT	United Kingdom Overseas Territories
UN	United Nations
UNCLOS	United Nations Convention on the Law of the Sea
UNCRC	United Nations Convention on the Rights of the Child
UNCTAD	United Nations Conference on Trade and Development
UNDRIP	United Nations Declaration on the Rights of Indigenous Peoples
UNEP	United Nations Environment Program
UNESCO	United Nations Educational, Scientific, and Cultural Organisation
UNFCCC	United Nations Framework Convention on Climate Change
UNGA	United Nations General Assembly
UNHCR	United Nations High Commissioner for Refugees
UNICEF	United Nations International Children's Emergency Fund
UNPKO	United Nations Peacekeeping Operations
UNSC	United Nations Security Council
UPU	Universal Postal Union
U.S.	United States
U.S.A.	United States of America

LIST OF ABBREVIATIONS

USAF	United States Armed Forces
USCDC	United States Centers for Disease Control and Prevention
USD	United States Dollar
USDOJ	United States Department of Justice
USFDA	United States Food and Drug Administration
USHMM	United States Holocaust Memorial Museum
USS	United States Ship
USSC	United States Supreme Court
USSEC	United States Securities and Exchange Commission
U.S.S.R.	Union of Soviet Socialist Republics
VIC	Victoria (Australia)
VMFA	Virginia Museum of Fine Arts
WA	Western Australia (Australia)
WB	World Bank
WCC	World Council of Churches
WEF	World Economic Forum
WFP	World Food Programme
WH	White House
WHO	World Health Organisation
WIPO	World Intellectual Property Organisation
WIR	World Investment Report
WMD	Weapons of Mass Destruction
WP	Warsaw Pact
WTC	World Trade Centre
WTO	World Trade Organisation
WWI	World War 1 (1914–1918)
WWII	World War 2 (1939–1945)
WWF	World Wide Fund for Nature
WWW	World Wide Web
YMCA	Young Men's Christian Association

Preface

This 500,000-word philosophical treatise is a four-volume collection of 1,094 philosophical stanzas that are arranged across eight chapters. The philosophical stanzas are comprised of fragments of thoughts, essays, doctrines, paragraphs, notes, short aphorisms, maxims, and propositions. The philosophical stanzas are systematically arranged across eight distinct chapters of:

1. Conventional Reality
2. Ultimate Reality
3. Classical Philosophy
4. Morality, Ethics, and Theology
5. Medicine
6. History and Jurisprudence
7. Politics, Diplomacy, and War
8. Commerce and Economics.

Volume I of the treatise contains Chapters 1 and 2, Volume II of the treatise contains Chapters 3 and 4, Volume III of the treatise contains Chapters 5 and 6, and last but not least, Volume IV of the treatise contains Chapters 7 and 8.

In this discourse, the author examines the contradictions of human nature, human existence, and reality; in the philosophical, psychological, medical, social, jurisprudential, historical, religious, economic, financial, metaphysical, political, and theological dimensions. The thoughts that I publish in this treatise are the precipitate of philosophical investigations that have occupied me for the great majority of the former eight years and nine months.

There is no established or over-arching empirical method of philosophical inquiry in this treatise. The fundamental essence of this qualitative discourse is to be an original, creative, and artistic work of philosophy, to aspire to be of an avant-garde nature, while attending to the millennia-old philosophical questions. Indeed, it is true that 'each age interprets and applies philosophy to its problems and aspirations', and that is precisely the grand objective of this philosophical treatise.[706]

Philosophy is the basic foundation of all human knowledge, and it is primarily responsible for the genesis and advancement of new academic disciplines such as the social and physical sciences. However, there exists no metaphysical (or physical) force that 'guarantees philosophical progress in any particular direction'.[707] This treatise promotes philosophical inquiry and discourse on classical and contemporary issues alike and engages the reader to contemplate for oneself, the multitude of Gordian knots inevitably resulting from life's existential questions.

Paul Baweja
the Commonwealth of Australia
September 2021

---

[706] Kenny, Anthony. (2010). *A New History of Western Philosophy*. New York: Oxford University Press, p. 8.

[707] Kenny, Anthony. (2010). *A New History of Western Philosophy*. New York: Oxford University Press, p. 6.

Keywords

Ancient, Being, Birth, Capital, Capitalism, Causality, Chaos, Communism, Conflict, Contemporary society, Convention, Conventional Reality, Corporation, Cosmos, Death, Debt, Desire, Determinism, Devil, Diplomacy, Discourse, Doctrine, Earth, Economics, Ego, Energy, Ethics, Evil, Freedom, Free-will, God, Good, History, Human civilisation, Idea, Ideology, Individualism, Institution, Jurisprudence, Justice, Karma, Law, Liberalism, Life, Materialism, Matter, Metaphysics, Modernity, Morality, Nation-state, Neoliberalism, New World, Non-Being, Order, Peace, Phenomenon, Phenomenal world, Philosophy, Politics, Poverty, Power, Private property, Profit, Religion, Revolution, Science, Slavery, Socialism, Sovereignty, Space, Theory, Time, Treaty, Ultimate Reality, Universe, War, Wealth, and Will.

This is a four volume treatise on philosophy.
This is the beginning of Volume III of IV.
The treatise is continued in Volume IV of IV.

Chapter 5

MEDICINE

'If someone wishes for good health,
one must first ask oneself if he is ready
to do away with the reasons for his illness.
Only then is it possible to help him.' [708]

HIPPOCRATES

---

708   Hippocrates. (ca. 460 BC – ca. 377 BC). See: Dew, Judith Lee. (2019). *Waking up from the Cancer Trance: The Truth about Preventing and Healing Cancer*. Victoria: Friesen Press, p. 58.

This chapter examines the natural philosophy of medicine in the contemporary modern civilised world. It considers the involuntary mechanical workings as effectuated by the autonomic nervous system of the human body; the ever-increasing *medicalisation* of social, moral, and ethical problems in the contemporary modern civilised society; and the associated despondency arising from the inevitability of human suffering. Not to mention, the certitude of death in the physical world.

959

Most of the human bodily processes that effectuate are unconscious to the human awareness. Come to understand that—in the conventional reality—humans exert minimal control over their material bodies.[709] As examples, consider that in the vicinity of 50-70 billion cells disintegrate each day in an adult human. In the human body, every second 2.5 million red blood cells meet their existential demise and are replaced. The average human adult heart beats around 60-100 beats per minute (BPM). The human body requires Oxygen (O) intake at the approximate quantity of 250 millilitres per minute; or 3.5 to 4.0 ml/kg/minute, of which a quarter is directed to the functioning of the human brain.

In addition, the pH level of the human blood stream is confined to the range of 7.35-7.45. In the event that the pH level rises above 7.45, a condition known as 'Alkalosis' occurs. Alternatively, in the

---

709   Consider the autonomic nervous system; which is responsible for the control of the human bodily functions that are not consciously directed; such as breathing, the heartbeat, and the digestive tract processes.

event that the pH level falls below 7.35, then a condition known as 'Acidosis' occurs. In the extreme case where the blood pH level rises above 7.8, or falls below 6.8, then the essential bonds that hold together critical proteins in cells can be destroyed, and death results.

Last but not least, the human spinal cord, which controls the primary intercommunication functions throughout the human body; connects the peripheral nervous system to the human brain and transmits nerve impulses through sensory neurons throughout the human body, to ensure the body's proper and systematic functioning.

Furthermore, the *Parasympathetic Nervous System* controls most of the major human bodily functions. Not to mention, that the biological determination of our genetic composition, that is, the unique human RNA and DNA code, and the twenty-four distinct human chromosomes contained within the deoxyribonucleic acid (DNA) molecule that are situated within the nucleus of the eukaryotic cell, are fixed through the course of the human life, and determine the gene 'potential' and 'expression' of this human life, these are matters that are beyond the human capacity and agency to consciously control.[710] Not to mention, that at the time of one's live birth, the human brain will, more or less, contain all the neurons it will ever have.

Also, our *dominant genes* transcend our recessive genes, to determine the visible human body traits of: skin pigmentation, hair colour, eye colour, blood type, *et cetera*. In addition, it is imperative to acknowledge the modern scientific fact that the human genome consists of ca. 3 billion DNA base pairs, which reside in the 23 pairs of chromosomes within the nucleus of all our cells.[711]

---

710 Mjoseth, Jeannine. (2017). *Sequencing all 24 human chromosomes uncovers rare disorders*. National Human Genome Research Institute. Date accessed: 10 March 2019. Access link: <https://www.genome.gov/news/news-release/Sequencing-all-24-human-chromosomes-uncovers-rare-disorders>

711 National Human Genome Research Institute. (2020). *Human Genome Project FAQ*. National Human Genome Research Institute. Date accessed: 24 November 2020. Access link: <https://www.genome.gov/human-genome-project/

Therefore, it is asserted with a high degree of confidence that humans are genetically conditioned to perceive the phenomenal world in a particular and distinct manner, prior to their live birth as a neonate on the Earth. Consider, does this not mean that you will subjectively experience the physical world from a particular perspective? Consequentially, what freedom do humans possess to think, act, and create their own conventional reality within the physical world, when a substantial majority of the human life is predetermined by genetic traits and biological composition?

960

How temporary is this existence of the human body in the physical world? When the heart ceases its involuntary rhythmic beating, cardiac arrest ensues, and a fatal heart attack can result in the human body's terminal demise. Within approximately three minutes of Oxygen (O) being deprived from the human brain, there can eventuate irreversible damage to the brain organ, and within five minutes this will result in permanent brain damage, and the real possibility of death becomes imminent.[712, 713]

961

In the twenty-first century, humans live in a modern civilised world, where there is an ever-increasing *medicalisation of social, ethical, and moral problems in human life*. The contemporary modern conventional society exhibits a scientific medicine-based approach to the resolution of non-medical issues in the modern

---

Completion-FAQ>
712   Villines, Zawn. (2016). *What Happens After A Lack of Oxygen to the Brain?* Spinal Cord. Date accessed: 25 March 2019. Access link: <https://www.spinalcord.com/blog/what-happens-after-a-lack-of-oxygen-to-the-brain>
713   Villines, Zawn. (2016). *What Happens After A Lack of Oxygen to the Brain?* Spinal Cord. Date accessed: 25 March 2019. Access link: <https://www.spinalcord.com/blog/what-happens-after-a-lack-of-oxygen-to-the-brain>

human life. That is a clinical and empirical approach, to treating psychological conditions and psychiatric disorders of the mind that are inherently metaphysical in their nature. That is to infer, the mental perturbations and psychological issues associated with the human existence are assigned a 'medical' and 'clinical' approach to their terminal resolution, comparable to the manner in which brain diseases of the nervous system are treated.

Furthermore, in respect to the clinical treatment of patients, the pharmaceutical industry and medical profession continually revise the standard medication doses for the on-going treatment of the existing medical conditions of presenting patients and their complaints and illnesses. In the majority of cases, this results in a *material increase in the quantity of medication* to be administered to humans as an instrumental aid to addressing modern mental illnesses (i.e., anxiety disorders, depression, eating disorders, personality disorders, autism spectrum disorder, and bipolar disorder), and psychological disorders (i.e., neurodevelopmental disorders, dissociative amnesia, dissociative identity disorder, somatic symptom disorder, neurocognitive disorders, histrionic personality disorder, and narcolepsy) in the modern human society.[714]

Inadvertently, as a result of the further consequential medical examination and the creation of experimental side effects on human patients in the contemporary modern society due to medication, this creates additional medical complications, which in turn requires incremental medication and medical treatment of the human patient in the modern civilised society. This results in a self-perpetuating and destructive cyclic endeavour, that nurtures the positive externality of a lucrative profitable enterprise for the pharmaceutical industry, until the terminal demise of the human patient in the physical world.

---

714 For a comprehensive list of the latest psychological and psychiatric disorders see: American Psychiatric Association. (2013). *Diagnostic and Statistical Manual of Menal Disorders (DSM-5)*. Fifth Edition. Virginia: American Psychiatric Association Publishing.

962

The contemporary advent of the birth control pill has liberated the libido (sex drive) of the female sex in the modern civilised world. For the female sex is now just as unconfined to engage in unrestricted copulation as the male sex in the modern conventional society. The *labium minus* has been liberated!

963

On the Inequity of the Global Burden of Disease. Universally, the pharmaceutical industry, the medical profession, and the government financial funding programs, collectively value and serve those who are members of the aristocratic socio-economic class of the highly-industrialised sovereign nation-states across the modern civilised world. The global pharmaceutical industry and institution of medicine direct the private donor contributions, public taxpayer funds, organisational research endeavours, government grants, and other organisational financial resources towards supporting the longevity of the elite and affluent socio-economic stratum of the modern civilised society in the OECD sovereign and independent nation-states. That is, directing resources, research, and funding towards alleviating the non-communicable diseases and diseases of affluence of the well lettered and opulent social class of the modern Western society.

The established for-profit medical corporations (i.e., Roche, Pfizer, Johnson & Johnson, Merck, Novartis, AbbVie, Takeda, Bristol-Myers Squibb, Sanofi, and Amgen) do not perceive invaluable economic feasibility in such financial resources being directed towards alleviating the miserable plight of the destitute and illiterate modern civilised humans in the poor third-world countries who suffer from negligible, treatable, and in some cases curable diseases (i.e., Respiratory disease, Diseases of the circulatory system, Diarrhea, Diphtheria, Measles, Poliomyelitis, Malnutrition, Malaria,

Tuberculosis, Tetanus, Pertussis, Neoplasms, and Lung cancer), in particular across the African continent.

Why does this the dismal reality exist in the twenty-first century modern civilised world? For there is no monetary, private, or economic interest in resolving the physical adversity and disproportionately high mortality rates of infants situated in the destitute third-world African nation-states.[715] Even though, on the balance of probabilities, a greater utilitarian moral good is derived from the saving of countless lives of the African children who are younger than 18 years old, and those people with a complete lifetime ahead of them, as opposed to saving the lives of people whom are older than 85 years of age in the industrialised, urbanised, privatised, and modernised first-world sovereign nation-states within the Western world. For the latter group have now lived and enjoyed their most capable and productive years of human life in the physical world. Whereas, the former group have an entire life that is yet to be experienced, yet to be lived, and yet to be cherished.

According to the International Policy Network's *Diseases of Poverty and the 10/90 Gap*' 2004 Report, 'activists claim that only 10 per cent of global health research is devoted to conditions that account for 90 per cent of the global disease burden—the so-called 10/90 Gap'.[716] The contemporary inequity in scientific research, public funding, and universal access to modern medicine for the

---

[715] According to the World Health Organisation (WHO), the risk of a child dying before reaching five years of age is still highest in the WHO African Region (76 per 1000 live births), around 8 times higher than that in the WHO European Region (9 per 1000 live births). Many countries still have very high under-five mortality rates—particularly those in WHO African Region, home to 5 of the 6 countries with an under-five years of age mortality rate above 100 deaths per 1000 live births. See: World Health Organisation. (2020). *Global Health Observatory (GHO) data. Under-five mortality*. World Health Organisation. Date accessed: 18 February 2020. Access link: <https://www.who.int/gho/child_health/mortality/mortality_under_five_text/en/>

[716] Stevens, Philip. (2004). *Diseases of poverty and the 10/90 Gap*. International Policy Network. Date accessed: 17 December 2020. Access link: <https://www.who.int/intellectualproperty/submissions/InternationalPolicyNetwork.pdf>

poor third-world nation-states, is resulting in the countless and needless preventable deaths of the African people in the twenty-first century.

However, the *laissez-faire* free-market ideology of capitalism and neo-liberalism, places a profound emphasis on the 'commerciality' and 'profitability' of products and services, far beyond the invaluable and immeasurable dimension of human life. That is the free-market positions a significant underlying concern on economic value; the market function of the 'invisible hand' that seeks out the greater financial utility of private profits and pecuniary gains.[717] These radical economic ideologies serve to uphold an artificial wealth distribution inequity across the human civilisation in the modern civilised world.

The trivial and superficial private quest for higher organisational profitability is of prime importance, prior to the public allocation and rendering of basic medical assistance to the global human population. Thus, in the process ensuring invaluable medical resources are not directed in terms of where they are likely to provide their greatest and maximal impact to save human lives. Not to mention, improve the universal standard of living of infants, young adults, and working age men and women across the modern civilised world, but rather where the direction of medical resources are most financially lucrative to seek ever higher returns on investment. The medical industry consciously targets its products and services to serve those human lives, that possess significant capital holdings, personal wealth, and private real property assets in the contemporary modern civilised world.

Thus, the pharmaceutical industry, in order to attract capital investment and best serve its shareholder's interests, remains in economic servitude to the affluent aristocratic constituents of the modern industrialised societies of the OECD sovereign nation-

---

717 Smith, Adam. (2006). *The Theory of Moral Sentiments*. Sao Paulo: MetaLibri, p. 165.

states, to meet the first-world national population public health needs as an organisational priority. This approach proves to be a more lucrative and commercial endeavour, as opposed to the eradication of preventable diseases that daily afflict the African people in Sub-Saharan Africa.

For the medical industry's pecuniary gains are the greatest to be exacted from the wealthy constituents of the modern industrialised society in the advanced first-world sovereign nation-states, as opposed to the vulnerable and destitute constituents of the U.N. Group of 77 member nation-states. It is a standard operable economic assumption of the capitalist modern civilised society, that the for-profit corporations are an artificial construct, without a social conscience and are fundamentally amoral in nature. However, the modern civilised humans are also increasingly exhibiting a similar, if not identical, demeanour themselves towards their fellow counterparts in the contemporary modern civilised society.

As an example, consider the global *Acquired Immune Deficiency Syndrome* (AIDS) epidemic at the latter stages of the twentieth century in the modern civilised world. Had it not been for the Republic of India's cosmopolitan, moral, humane, ethical, and utopian conscience in the early twenty-first century, through its manufacturing of generic drugs, several hundred thousand African and Asian people would have surely perished on the Earth.[718]

Private pharmaceutical drug companies and medical research corporations predominantly exist to further and protect their private copyrights, profits, trade secrets, registered patents, trademarks, innovation of medicines, and ensure high revenues from original brand-name drugs by the prevention of generic products from entering and competing on the global pharmaceutical drug market.

---

718 The Economic Times. (2016). 80% drugs to combat AIDS supplied by India: JP Nadda. The Economic Times. Date accessed: 13 December 2019. Access link: <https://economictimes.indiatimes.com/industry/healthcare/biotech/healthcare/80-drugs-to-combat-aids-supplied-by-india-jp-nadda/articleshow/52671827.cms>

The ultimate aim that underpins this unconscionable corporate conduct is to ensure that the company's shareholders economic and financial interests remain intact and secure, even at the moral and ethical costs of hundreds and thousands of preventable human deaths across the continents of Africa and Asia.[719]

Furthermore, as an additional and supplementary example, consider the introduction of the *Trade-Related Aspects of Intellectual Property Rights (TRIPS) Agreement* in the World Trade Organisation (WTO) in 1995. The TRIPS Agreement is an enforceable instrument of the international law designed to institutionalise the global governance of intellectual property rights protection in the modern civilised world. Ultimately, such an international agreement would be most detrimental to the least developed third-world countries, that possess large populations, and are marked by a higher degree of material poverty, have an under-developed national health care system, lack adequate public infrastructure, and demonstrate lower levels of completed elementary school education amongst the national population.

For the industrialised, urbanised, privatised, and modernised, first-world Western nation-states to insist that the United Nations *Group of 77* poor nation-states, whose illiterate, malnourished, and destitute national populations cannot afford water, food, education, public transport, electricity, clothing, residential housing, and basic access to health and dental care, that these backward, wayward, and poor sovereign nation-states equally implement and comply with a rigorous global intellectual property regime is wholly against and so far removed from the egalitarian principles of social justice, ethical awareness, eternal law, and natural law—devoid of moral conscience and the basic principles of morality—that it beggars belief.

The legal fact that the for-profit corporations are amoral and indifferent to the social, psychological, as well as the ethical and

---

719   Bhalla, Nita. (2011). *Millions will die if India stops AIDS drugs: U.N.* Reuters. Date accessed: 29 March 2019. Access link: <https://www.reuters.com/article/us-india-aids-drugs-idUSTRE7643U120110705>

moral problems of the constituents of the modern human society is a conventional reality of the modern civilised world. The behemoth of multinational pharmaceutical corporations are not utilitarian in their corporate endeavours in the modern civilised world. Such private corporations do not exist to maximise the 'public good' from their commercial and trading activities, nor are such artificial for-profit entities established for a benevolent, philanthropic, charitable, altruistic, or humanitarian purpose. However, these private corporations are exclusively concerned with the maximisation of organisational profits for their shareholders financial interests.

What has become of humanity, even at the moral question of the life and death of our fellow humans suffering from the AIDS medical condition in the contemporary modern civilised world? As an individualistic, neoliberal, secular, atheist, commercialised, contractualised, Westernised, Anglicised, Europeanised, privatised, liberalised, globalised, and capitalist modern civilised society, the modern human civilisation stands all too ready to affirm their counterparts' deaths, in order to protect intangible corporate assets; inventions, registered patents, trade secrets, profits, trademarks, and copyrights.

What is the transcendental purpose of such scientific and medical advancements in the modern civilised world, if they cannot be effectuated into their proper, noble, and righteous moral utilitarian function? Namely, to save the life of an individual suffering from a treatable and curable disease in the modern civilised world. However, the dismal and unethical reality of the conventional reality is that the shameful and egotistical humans, first seek the narrow advancement, the private security of their egotistical and self-interested economic gains; profit maximisation and pecuniary gains, prior to the universal achievement of the greatest 'public good'—the saving of as many human lives as possible in the modern civilised world, not to mention, the alleviation of curable pain and unnecessary suffering across the human civilisation.

In the event that an ordinary citizen cannot afford the market equilibrium price of the required medication to sustain one's life in the contemporary modern civilised world, and unless the federal government of that particular sovereign nation-state is prepared to financially intervene, in order to publicly subsidise the cost of expensive brand medicines, and thereby, artificially decrease the product price of modern medicine on the pharmaceutical market, then that impoverished particular individual must die in vain.

The private security of financial profits and economic gains, at the expense of human life, is the dismal and immoral state of the twenty-first century modern civilised society. The contemporary case of the AIDS epidemic best demonstrates the egoistic baseness of human nature. That is to say, the positioning of corporate profits is ahead of humanity's greater welfare in the physical world; the near universal prevalence of greed over generosity.

964

Medicine is the science of the adjournment of death; however, death is ultimately inevitable. *Contra vim mortis non crescit herba in hortis* (no herb grows in the gardens against the power of death).

965

The respiration of the human body cannot be controlled indefinitely; it is an involuntary act of the Autonomic Nervous System. Humans do not consciously determine to inhale Oxygen or exhale Carbon Dioxide vis-à-vis the *Pulmōnis* (lungs), humans do not exercise free-will in this respect. For if humans were to attempt otherwise, and the brain consciously determined to cease the natural rhythmic respiration process, it would inevitably result in the cessation, the existential demise, of human life.[720] As an example, consider is the

---

720 'the will in many ways acts blindly; as in all those functions of our body which

voluntary cessation of respiration a plausible, logical, and rational outcome in the exercise of human free-will, in that you forcefully, unethically, and immorally, determine to no longer remain conventionally existent within the domain of the physical world?

966

The human body is a conventionally existent entity of disease.[721]

---

are not guided by knowledge, in all its vital and vegetative processes, digestion, circulation, secretion, growth, and reproduction. Not only the actions of the body, but the whole body itself, as was shown above, is phenomenon of the will'. See: Schopenhauer, Arthur. (E. F. J. Payne, Trans.) (1969). *The World as Will and Representation*. Volume I. New York: Dover Publications, p. 115.

721 Consider the following known medical conditions and diseases, which are by no means exhaustive: Acquired Immune Deficiency Syndrome, African Trypanosomiasis, Ainhum, Alzheimer's Disease, Amebic Dysentery, Anemia, Anorexia Nervosa, Anthrax, Apoplexy and Stroke, Arboviruses, Arenaviruses, Arthritis (Rheumatoid), Ascariasis, Bacillary Dysentry, Beriberi, Black Death, Black and Brown Lung Disease, Bleeding Disorders, Botulism, Brucellosis (Malta Fever and Undulant Fever), Bubonic Plague, Cancer, Carrion's Disease (Oraya Fever), Catarrh, Cestode Infection, Chagas' Disease, Chlorosis, Cholera, Cirrhosis, Clonorchiasis, Croup, Cystic Fibrosis, Cytomegalovirus Infection, Dengue, Diabetes, Diarrheal Diseases (Acute), Diphtheria, Down Syndrome, Dracunculiasis, Dropsy, Dysentery, Dyspepsia, Ebola Virus Disease, Echinococcosis (Hydatidosis), Eclampsia, Emphysema, Encephalitis Lethargica, Enterobiasis, Epilepsy, Ergotism, Erysipelas, Fascioliasis, Fasciolopsiasis, Favism, Filariasis, Fungus Infections (Mycoses), Fungus Poisoning, Gallstones (Cholelithiasis), Gangrene, Genetic Disease, Giardiasis, Glomerulonephritis (Bright's Disease), Goiter, Gonorrhea, Gout, Heart-Related Diseases, Herpes Simplex, Herpesviruses, Histoplasmosis, Hookworm Infection, Huntington's Disease (Chorea), Hypertension, Infectious Hepatitis, Infectious Mononucleosis, Inflammatory Bowel Disease (Crohn's Disease, Ulcerative Colitis), Influenza, Japanese B Encephalitis, Lactose Intolerance and Malabsorption, Lassa Fever, Lead Poisoning, Legionnaires' Disease (Legionellosis, Pontiac Fever, Legionella Pneumonia), Leishmaniasis, Leprosy (Hansen's Disease), Leptospirosis, Leukemia, Lupus Erythematosus, Lyme Borreliosis (Lyme Disease), Malaria, Marburg Virus Disease, Mastoiditis, Measles, Meningitis, Milk Sickness (Tremetol Poisoning), Multiple Sclerosis, Mumps, Muscular Dystrophy, Myasthenia Gravis, Nematode Infection, Onchocerciasis, Ophthalmia (Trachoma, Conjunctivitis), Osteoarthritis, Osteoporosis, Paget's Disease of Bone, Paragonimiasis, Parkinson's Disease, Pellagra, Periodontal Disease (Pyorrhea), Pica, Pinta, Plague of Athens, Pneumocystis Pneumonia (Interstitial Plasma Cell Pneumonia, Pneumocystosis), Pneumonia, Poliomyelitis, Protein-

967

Humans exert minimal self-control over the phenomenon of the human body. Most bodily functions are effectuated without their conscious awareness, voluntary consent, or conscious process of cognition. As examples, consider the human digestion of food through the gastrointestinal tract, the passage of fluids through the kidneys, and the excretion of bodily wastes and bowel movements through the large and small intestines. In addition, the human brain emits signals via the spinal cord and into the nerve endings of the human body to effectuate its instructions, without conscious human affirmation, self-determination, or immediate intervention.

In fact, the human brain (see Figure 40) is the most complex organ in the human body; it contains approximately 86 billion nerve cells (i.e., neurons).[722] Furthermore, each individual neuron can form connexions with tens of thousands of other proximate neurons within the human brain, to form distinct neural pathways via axons and dendrites, resulting in the creation of synapses within the human brain. Beyond the astronomical quantum of neurons, the human brain contains glial cells; the quantum of which is several times greater than the neurons within the human brain.

Energy Malnutrition, Protozoan Infection, Puerperal Fever, Q Fever, Rabies, Relapsing Fever, Rheumatic Fever and Rheumatic Heart Disease, Rickets and Osteomalacia, Rickettsial Diseases, Rocky Mountain Spotted Fever and Related Diseases, Rubella, Saint Anthony's Fire, Scarlet Fever, Schistosomiasis, Scrofula, Scurvy, Sickle-Cell Anemia, Smallpox, Streptococcal Diseases, Strongyloidiasis, Sudden Infant Death Syndrome, Sudden Unexplained Death Syndrome, Sweating Sickness, Syphilis, Syphilis Nonveneral, Tapeworm Infection, Tay-Sachs Disease, Tetanus, Tetanus Neonatal, Tatany, Toxoplasmosis, Trematode Infection, Trench Fever, The Treponematoses, Trichinosis, Trichuriasis, Tuberculosis, Tularemia, Typhoid Fever, Typhomalarial Fever, Typhus Epidemic, Typhus Murine, Typhus Scrub, Urolithiasis, Varicella-Zoster Virus Disease, Whooping Cough, Yaws, and Yellow Fever.

722 Herculano-Houzel, Suzana. (2009). The human brain in numbers: a linearly scaled-up primate brain. *Frontiers in Human Neuroscience*. November 2009, Volume 3, Article 31, p. 6.

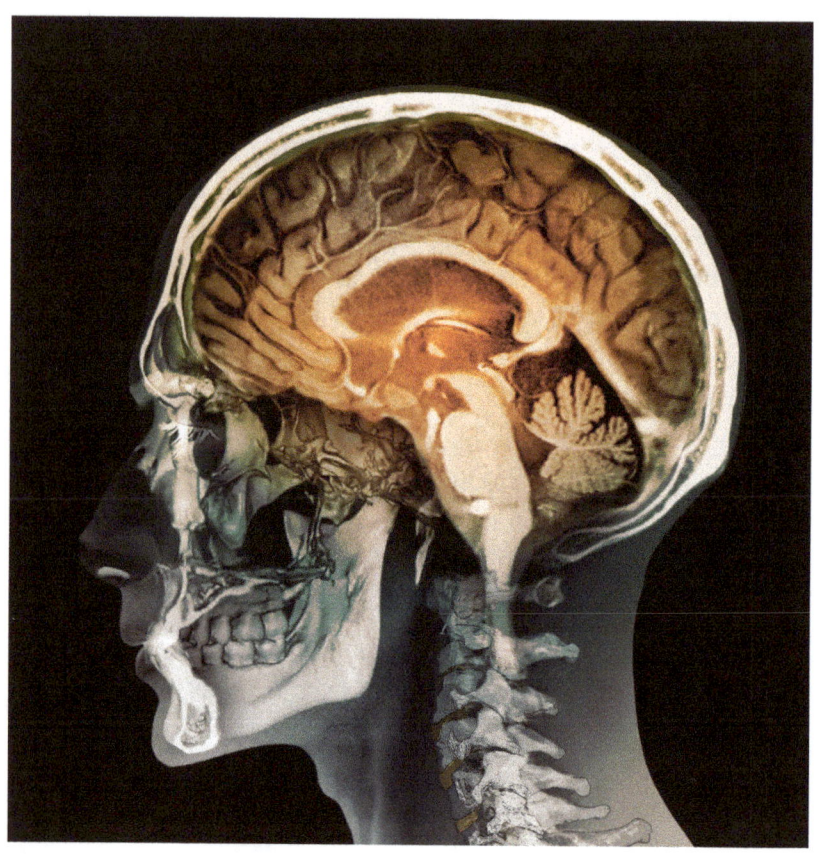

Figure 40: Human head, MRI, and 3D CT scans.
Image Credit: Zephyr / Science Photo Library.

In sum, the brain is the single most sophisticated human body organ that comes to shape, define, and create the human perception of the phenomenal world.[723] Not to negate or devalue the biological fact that genes are largely responsible for the formation of brain structure, and how the brain ages through the course of human life. Thereby, adding to the argument of *Determinism*, that how humans come to perceive the phenomenal world, has, in substantial form, already been determined, outside of the bounds of one's fictitious free-will and finite personal agency, to perceive the conventional reality otherwise.

Indeed, a grand and unprecedented scientific project; the *Human Connectome Project* sponsored by the U.S. National Institute of Health (NIH), is achieving leaps and bounds in the scientific human understanding of the most complex organ of the human body—the human brain. According to the Human Connectome Project's official website:

> '*The Human Connectome Project is designed to construct a map of the complete structural and functional neural connections in vivo within and across individuals. The project represents the first large-scale attempt to collect and share data of a scope and detail sufficient to begin the process of addressing deeply fundamental questions about human connectional anatomy and variation.*' [724]

Furthermore, distinct parts and regions of the human body are impacted by the release of hormones, chemicals, and neurotransmitters, which in turn, influence human psychology and behaviour towards other people in the human society, and one's

---

723 For further information on the development of the human brain, see: Tierney, Adrienne L., and Nelson, Charles A. (2009). Brain Development and the Role of Experience in the Early Years. *Zero Three*. November 1, Volume 30, No. 2, pp. 9–13.

724 Human Connectome Project. (2020). *Human Connectome Project: About*. Human Connectome Project. Date accessed: 19 February 2020. Access link: <http://www.humanconnectomeproject.org/about/>

personal perception of the physical world. In addition, the human autonomic nervous system, which is comprised of the sympathetic and parasympathetic nervous systems is in control of the physical human body and psychological cognitive processes without our entire conscious awareness.[725]

968

On Cloning and Gene-editing. The fields of modern science, medicine, biotechnology and genetic engineering have all made monumental progress over the former three decades (1990–2020), however, there remain serious ethical, moral, theological, religious, and legal questions to consider, let alone terminally resolve, prior to the ultimate scientific fiction idea of the whole creation of completely artificial humans, which are scientifically engineered, becoming a conventional reality in the modern civilised world.

The very idea of completely artificial humans that are scientifically engineered is not an impossible endeavour. Let us examine some of the major cloning and genetic engineering advances in the field of biology. For example, consider the creation of 'Dolly the Sheep' in 1996; the modern world's first cloned sheep in Scotland, the United Kingdom of Great Britain and Northern Ireland (see Figure 41).[726] In addition, investigate the creation of 'Snuppy' in 2005; the modern world's first successfully cloned Afghan hound in Seoul, South Korea (see Figure 42).[727]

---

[725] The Autonomic Nervous System (ANS) controls internal body processes such as the following: blood pressure, heart and breathing rates, body temperature, digestion, metabolism, the balance of water (pH levels) and electrolytes (i.e., sodium and calcium) and the production of body fluids (i.e., saliva, sweat, and tears), urination, defecation, and the sexual response.

[726] Weintraub, Karen. (2016). *20 Years after Dolly the Sheep Led the Way—Where Is Cloning Now?* The Scientific American. Date accessed: 27 November 2020. Access link: <https://www.scientificamerican.com/article/20-years-after-dolly-the-sheep-led-the-way-where-is-cloning-now/>

[727] Latson, Jennifer. (2015). *What Happened to the First Cloned Puppy.* Time Magazine. Date accessed: 27 November 2020.

CHAPTER 5 | MEDICINE

Figure 41: Dolly was the world's first cloned sheep.
Image Credit: Science Photo Library / Alamy.

Figure 42: Snuppy, right, the first cloned Afghan hound,
next to his genetic father.
Image Credit: Seoul National University / Getty Images.

Furthermore, and most concerningly, examine the case of the Chinese scientist Dr. He Jiankui, who conducted 'gene-editing on human embryos' in 2018. This contemporary scientific work resulted in the birth of twin girls (known by their pseudonyms 'Lulu' and 'Nana') with edited genomes in the People's Repubic of China.[728] There are serious ethical and moral questions that need to be vigorously and publicly debated prior to the commonplace scientific engineering of mutations into human embryos, which are subsequently utilised to create genetically modified human offspring.[729]

969

On Genetics. Human genes come to determine human life within the physical world. At the exact moment of fertilisation, when the spermatozoon and the ovum amalgamate, to form a diploid cell, the future neonate's genetic composition is completely determined; including the sex of the infant. Beyond the type of sex, genetics also have a significant involvement in the determination a human's capacity for intelligence, personality type, eye colour, hair colour, skin pigmentation, and height.

Furthermore, our genetic material performs an integral part in the onset of medical conditions and diseases in life. That is to say, genetic disorders are diseases that are caused by a change in the DNA sequence. Such disorders arise by a mutation in a single gene (i.e., a monogenic disorder), or by mutations in multiple genes (i.e., multifactorial inheritance disorder). Common genetic

---

Access link: <https://time.com/3822573/snuppy/>

728 Rana, Preetika. (2019). *How a Chinese Scientist Broke the Rules to Create the First Gene-Edited Babies.* The Wall Street Journal. Date accessed: 17 December 2020. Access link: <https://www.wsj.com/articles/how-a-chinese-scientist-broke-the-rules-to-create-the-first-gene-edited-babies-11557506697>

729 Cyranoski, David. (2019). *The CRISPR-baby scandal: what's next for human gene-editing.* Nature. Date accessed: 27 November 2020. Access link: <https://www.nature.com/articles/d41586-019-00673-1>

disorders include, but are not limited to: Colon Cancer, Crohn's Disease, Cystic Fibrosis, Dercum Disease, Fragile X Syndrome, Gaucher Disease, Wilson's Disease, Thalassemia, Turner Syndrome, Velecardiofacial Syndrome, Porphyria, Retinitis Pigmentosa, Charcot-Marie Tooth Disease, Sickle Cell Disease, Klinefelter Syndrome, Holoprosencephaly, and Tay-Sachs Disease.

970

On sexism as it relates to language in the Anglo-Saxon modern medicine canon. The medical notation for a female's genitalia in Latin is termed *pudendum,* translated into English; this equates to 'whereof one ought to feel shame'. Clearly, this is most demonstrable of fundamental male sexism towards the female sex, where the white Anglo-Saxon male physician of the fourteenth century has equated, titled, and connotated, the female's genitals with the eternal and ignoble feelings of guilt and shame in the conventional human society.

In addition, the educational material provisioned in the contemporary modern medicine textbooks is reflective of institutionalised sexism towards women in the conventional modern civilised society. This creates the perception of a 'female medical subject' to be physically perused for medical examination, which, in turn, portrays the perpetual perspective of masculinity and male domination within the medical profession of the modern civilised society.[730] A sexist perspective that all too often illustrates

---

730   See: Dijkstra, Anja F., Verdonk, Petra., and Lagro-Janssen, Antoine L.M. (2008). Gender bias in medical textbooks: examples from coronary heart disease, depression, alcohol abuse and pharmacology. *Medical Education.* Volume 42, pp. 1021–1028.
Morgan, Susan., Plaisant, Odile., Lignier, Baptiste., and Moxham, Bernard J. (2013). Sexism and anatomy, as discerned in textbooks and as perceived by medical students at Cardiff University and University of Paris Descartes. *Journal of Anatomy.* Volume 224, No. 3, pp. 352–365.
Levinson, Richard. (1976). Sexism in Medicine. *The American Journal of Nursing.* Volume 76, No. 3, pp. 426–431.

a male physician and a female patient in a clinical setting.[731] In a broader societal context, this sexist conventional reality represents and reflects the socio-economic class, personal status, reputation, influence, financial assets, private wealth, personal income, formal education, private property, and political power disparities between the male sex and the female sex in the contemporary modern civilised society.[732]

---

[731] Saner, Emine. (2019). *A textbook case of sexism in medicine?* The Guardian. Date accessed: 13 September 2019. Access link: <https://www.theguardian.com/world/shortcuts/2019/sep/10/orthopaedic-medical-textbook-sexism-caroline-criado-perez>
Leach, Maddison. (2019). *University medical textbook branded 'soft porn'*. Nine Honey. Date accessed: 21 September 2019. Access link: <https://honey.nine.com.au/latest/soft-porn-university-medical-textbook-twitter-slammed/0741c17e-63b9-45ea-8c02-f8654f87ef2e>

[732] Duncan, Elly. (2019). *Doctors are calling out these 'objectifying' medical textbooks.* SBS Australia. Date accessed: 21 September 2019. Access link: <https://www.sbs.com.au/news/the-feed/doctors-are-calling-out-these-objectifying-medical-textbooks>

Chapter 6

HISTORY AND JURISPRUDENCE

'At his best, man is the noblest of all animals; separated from law and justice he is the worst.' [733]

ARISTOTLE

---

[733] Aristotle. (ca. 384 BC – ca. 322 BC). See: Aristotle. (Benjamin Jowett, Trans.) (1997). *Politics*. Book 1. The Constitution Society. Date accessed: 12 September 2019. Access link: <https://www.constitution.org/ari/polit_01.htm>

This chapter examines the natural philosophy of positive law within the apparatus of the modern sovereign nation-state. It investigates the establishment of positive laws by a royal sovereign (i.e., rule by royal decree), and examines the institutions of president and prime minister within civil governments (i.e., statutes, executive orders, prime minister's directive, and acts of parliament), not to mention, the elected members of a sovereign parliament who occupy powerful positions of high public office within the sovereign and independent nation-state; elected representatives of the people that hold key positions in established institutions (i.e., the high court, the supreme court, the federal parliament, the defence and foreign ministry, *et cetera*), that promote legal and civil influence in the sovereign nation-state, and provision political power to assert lawful and legitimate authority within the territorial demarcation of a nation-state.

Consequently, this chapter considers authoritarian political leaders and civil governments legitimisation and sanctioning of the 'use of force' in the enactment and enforcement of unjust positive laws within the defined territory of the sovereign and independent nation-state.

Parallel to the philosophical analysis of positive law, this chapter also investigates the philosophy of human action and moral conduct in the modern history; as established by the tenets of natural law. It investigates how *Saint Thomas Aquinas' Natural Law Theory* has been misappropriated by the Western civilisation (i.e., the Anglo-American, British, and European civilisations) in the modern era to create and institutionalise an oppressive Western political and financial world order that is based on the collective ideologies of imperialism, liberalism, republicanism, colonialism, neoliberalism, mercantilism, racism, proslavery, Christian proselytising, and capitalism. A new Western world order that is predominantly oppressive for the Arab, African, and Asian civilisations. Furthermore, *Saint Augustine's Doctrine of Natural Law* is also examined in respect to its application against human made positive laws within the conventional modern society.

In addition, this chapter also explores the mainstream and conventional practice of gender inequality and patriarchy institutionalised throughout the annals of human history, and how patriarchy began to disintegrate with the contemporary social, legal, economic, civil rights, and political reforms over the course of the last 300 years. Fundamental political, legal, social, and economic changes in the modern civilised world, which are part of the greater ideological struggle of feminism which demonstrated its modern genesis in the seventeenth century, from which point in time the feminist ideological movement went from strength to strength with monumental shifts beginning to effectuate into international support and recognition for the cause of women's rights movements, ultimately, culminating into the universal women's suffrage movement in the nineteenth century. The chapter also considers the Anglo-Saxon and European civilisations lawful discrimination and unprecedented genocide of the Indigenous civilisations throughout the Commonwealth of Australia, the Dominion of Canada, New Zealand, and the United States of America.

Last but not least, this chapter inquiries into war and conflict as an unalterable dimension of the human condition within the physical world, notwithstanding, the constraining mechanism and institutions of 'positive law' and 'natural morality' within the conventional reality. Finally, the chapter also considers the institutionalisation of novel theological doctrine and political ideology to psychologically condition and govern the human population, towards fundamental perspectives of the conventional reality.

CHAPTER 6 | HISTORY AND JURISPRUDENCE

At the fundamental core of the concept of law is the universal idea of natural justice; however, the forces of the philosophy of law and the history of law do not always reconcile in the physical world. As this chapter shall demonstrate, that while the ancient institution of law can be traced as far back as His Majesty King Hammurabi's *Code of Laws*, the ideal universal state of just peace and blind justice are far from the realisation and rational capacity of the human civilisation.

971

This stanza postulates an avant-garde philosophical doctrine: '*The Naturalisation of Radical Ideology into the Conventional Society*'. This doctrine asserts that what is presently considered mainstream in the human society, at a select antecedent period in the human history, represented heterodoxy, but for the radical change. That is change against the established and institutionalised norms and customs of that traditional, orthodox, and conservative contemporary social, economic, and political order, that such envisioned fundamental change would not have effectuated, materialised, and transpired in the [particular] sovereign nation-state, or the [universal] modern civilised world. This philosophical doctrine holds valid and constant throughout the annals of the human civilisation.

The philosophical doctrine expounded by this thesis is eternally true. For example, consider the infamous trial of Galileo Galilei (1564–1642) in the year 1633 resulting in Galilei's successful conviction of heresy, when the Roman Catholic Church refused to accept his empirical evidence-based findings that were postulated upon observable phenomenon and scientific fact—that the Earth revolves around the Sun. In addition, consider the example of the constitutional and legislative enactment of the belated legal right of the Aboriginal Australians to vote in the Commonwealth of

Australia in 1962.[734] The Aboriginal Australians' right to vote was further affirmed by the overwhelming egalitarian goodwill of the Australian people; 90.8 per cent of Australians to be precise, who voted 'Yes' on the political basis of the official referendum held in 1967.[735] Thereby, granting Aboriginal Australian's citizenship and affording them the legal right to vote at the Federal / Commonwealth elections vis-à-vis constitutional reform.[736]

Throughout the annals of human history, it is evidenced time and time again, that what once was, upon inception, considered radical, in the future can become mainstream. Be it the period of several years, or three hundred and fifty-nine years later, when the Roman Catholic Church acceded in 1992, under the leadership of Pope John Paul II (1920–2005), when the Church finally acquiesced that Galileo Galilei's original academic contribution to human knowledge in the field of Astronomy was factually correct. That is Galileo's scientific hypothesis of the Earth revolving around the Sun in the Solar System was intellectually justified and proven as a truthful and factual empirical observation.[737] However, the 1633

---

734 In 1962, the Menzies Government amended the *Commonwealth Electoral Act* to give Indigenous Australian people the right to enrol and vote in Commonwealth elections irrespective of their voting rights at the state level.

735 Department of the Parliamentry Library. (2002). *Parliamentary Handbook of the Commonwealth of Australia*. 29th Edition, Canberra: Parliamentary Library, p. 563.

736 A Referendum approved Commonwealth Constitutional change. Section 127 of the Australian Constitution was removed in its entirety. This amendment allowed Indigenous Australians to be counted in the Commonwealth Census. Section 51 of the Constitution was amended to allow the Commonwealth to make 'special laws' for Indigenous people. Both Houses of the Parliament passed the proposed Act unanimously; consequently, a 'No' case was not submitted. More than 90 per cent of Australians registered a 'Yes' vote with all six Commonwealth states voting in favour of the constitutional amendment. See: Australian Electoral Commission. (2019). *Electoral milestones for Indigenous Australians*. Australian Electoral Commission. Date accessed: 28 July 2019. Access link: <https://www.aec.gov.au/Indigenous/milestones.htm>

737 Cowell, Alan. (1992). *After 350 Years, Vatican Says Galileo Was Right: It Moves*. The New York Times. Date accessed: 28 July 2019. Access link: <https://www.nytimes.com/1992/10/31/world/after-350-years-vatican-says-galileo-was-right-it-moves.html>

Roman Inquisition's proceedings and legal trial of Galileo were a demonstration of the Roman Catholic Church's unchecked and unquestioned power in modern Europe; a power that corrupted the progress and betterment of the human civilisation.

Yet the relinquishment of power; political, legal, religious, and economic power does not eventuate without the first category of heretics and radicals that are to become the founding martyrs for their then fundamental ideas and revisionist perceptions of the physical world. In fact, John Badby (see Figure 43), John Wycliffe, Walter Lollard, Sir John Oldcastle (see Figure 44), and John Huss, represent classic examples of the possession and expression of fundamental ideas. Radical ideas that are contrary to the then conventional Catholic beliefs and practices of the conventional human society, based on the contemporary religious order of the fourteenth century Europe. Ultimately, it took a 500-year period of the human civilisation for the Roman Catholic Church to cede legal, religious, social, economic, and political control, and relinquish the Western civilisation from the exertion of its seething iron-clad hold on human affairs in the conventional European society.

In addition, consider the institution of human slavery in British North America, which was at its peak, from 1619 to 1863, when the Anglo-Saxon Americans engaged in the *Atlantic Slave Trade* across the Atlantic Ocean. In the modern civilised Western world, slavery was institutionalised and embedded in all material aspects of the American conventional society for approximately three consecutive generations. The human-constructed U.S. institutions, such as the U.S. Senate, the U.S. House of Representatives, the U.S. Government, the U.S. Congress, the U.S. White House, the U.S. Supreme Court, the U.S. Armed Forces, the U.S. National Guard, and the U.S. public school education system, came to legalise, uphold, and reinforce the radical ideology of proslavery as a legitimate legal right of the white, male, and Christian Anglo-Saxon American people.

Historical examples of the U.S. positive laws; Presidential Executive Orders, acts of the U.S. Congress, and judge-made case

Figure 43: John Badby being burned in a barrel at St. Bartholomew's in Smithfield for heresy as a Lollard in 1410.
Image Credit: Chronicle / Alamy.

Figure 44: The English Lollard Leader Sir John Oldcastle being burned in St. Giles in the Fields for insurrection and Lollard heresy in 1417.
Image Credit: Chronicle / Alamy.

law, collectively provision immutable proof of the institutionalisation and regulation of human slavery in the United States of America. For example, consider the *Virginia Slave Act of 1705*, the *Fugitive Slave Act of 1793*, the *Slave Trade Act of 1794*, and not to mention, the U.S. Chief Justice Roger Brooke Taney's majority opinion on behalf of the U.S. Supreme Court that delivered the following immoral and illegitimate statement in the legal case concerning *Dred Scott v. Sandford* (1857) … 'The Negro might justly and lawfully be reduced to slavery for his benefit'.[738]

The modern civilised world's history demonstrates that it is self-evident the Western civilisation has discarded its own philosophical and moral tenets, not to mention, it has abandoned the exercise of human conscience, on the subject matter of the function of just positive laws in the body politic. The Western civilisation has refuted Saint Augustine's Ideal of Positive Law; that 'An unjust law is no law at all', and transgressed Saint Aquinas' Philosophy of Natural Justice; 'An unjust law is a human law that is not rooted in eternal law and natural law.[739] Any law that uplifts human personality is just. Any law that degrades human personality is unjust'.[740]

It is an inevitable fact that human-made institutions are subject to bias, corruption, racism, decay, antagonism, discrimination, and prejudice. In fact, such artificial institutions are only a reflection of the composition of the constituents situated within them at any given point in time. At the time of the U.S. President Abraham Lincoln's *Proclamation of Emancipation* in 1863, the ideal notion of a free black African Negro in the Confederate States of America was

---

738 Circuit Court of the United States of America. (1857). *Dred Scott v Sandford. Chief Justice Taney (Opinion of the Court)*. Date accessed: 5 February 2019. Access link: <http://teachingamericanhistory.org/library/document/dred-scott-v-sandford/>

739 In: Martin Luther King Jr. Letter from Birmingham City Jail in: *A Testament of Hope: The Essential Writings and Speeches of Martin Luther King Jr.* (1991) James Melvin Washington Edition. New York: Harper Collins, pp. 48–49.

740 In: Sturm, Douglas. (1984). Crisis in the American Republic: The Legal and Political Significance of Martin Luther King's 'Letter from a Birmingham Jail'. *Journal of Law and Religion*. Volume 2, No. 2, pp. 315–316.

considered fundamental, radical, and extreme; unprecedented in all great respects of the white Christian Anglo-American man's utopian society.[741]

Lest we forget, the great U.S. Founding Father, and the third U.S. President Thomas Jefferson (r. 1801–1809) possessed more than 600 black African Negro slaves.[742] Yes, that is the same Thomas Jefferson who asserted and proclaimed in the preamble of the *U.S. Declaration of Independence 1776*; … 'We hold these truths to be self-evident, that all men are created equal, that they are endowed by their Creator with certain unalienable Rights, that among these are Life, Liberty, and the Pursuit of Happiness'.[743]

The immoral and inhumane act of the U.S. President Thomas Jefferson degrading the free black African Negro human to the institution of slavery is not an anomaly, for it was a common and conventional reality that was demonstrated by several of the U.S. Founding Fathers, not to mention, the U.S. Presidents; James Monroe, George Washington, James K. Polk, and Andrew Johnson. Thus, it should also be of no surprise that it is also a self-evident truth that the United States of America was founded and built upon the immoral instutions of genocide, slavery, oppression, and racism—crimes against humanity.

The United States' President Abraham Lincoln (r. 1861–1865) (see Figure 45) is the greatest political leader in the modern history of the Western civilisation. For it is the U.S. President Lincoln who single-handedly, against American, British, and European national opinion, was able to politically, economically, socially, militarily,

---

741 The Confederacy was originally formed by seven secessionist slave-holding states: South Carolina, Mississippi, Florida, Alabama, Georgia, Louisiana, and Texas.
742 Mann, Lina. (2020). *The Enslaved Household of President Thomas Jefferson*. The White House Historical Association. Date accessed: 21 October 2020. Access link: <https://www.whitehousehistory.org/slavery-in-the-thomas-jefferson-white-house>
743 U.S. National Archives. (2020). *Declaration of Independence: A Transcription*. U.S. National Archives. Date accessed: 21 October 2020. Access link: <https://www.archives.gov/founding-docs/declaration-transcript>

CHAPTER 6 | HISTORY AND JURISPRUDENCE

Figure 45: The 16th U.S. President Abraham Lincoln.
Image Credit: U.S. National Archives / Alamy.

and diplomatically re-condition the free white Catholic Irish man, the English Protestant Puritans, the Ulster Scots, the Quakers, and the British Crown persecuted Anglo-Saxon and English religious minorities, who fled the Kingdom of Great Britain to the North American continent in the sixteenth century, to collectively, fight and die for the freedom of the unequal black African Negro slave in the nineteenth century (i.e., in the course of the *American Civil War* 1861–1865).

In practical effect, it was the U.S. President Abraham Lincoln who dismantled the 300-year-old U.S. institution of human slavery. This was achieved in an era when the black African Negro was a lawful human slave; a market commodity who was commonly shot dead for the colour of the Negro's black skin, whipped, beaten, lynched, treated beneath the dignity of human life, like an insignificant and inconsequential item of indentured property able to be freely traded on domestic and international markets. The modern life of a black African Negro slave was most comparable to international trade in animals, plant species, and the natural commodities of sugar, coffee, tobacco, rum, tea, oil, rubber, cotton, silk, wheat, rice, and cocoa in the early modern civilised world. Regrettably, the historical reality of the United States' establishment is founded on the fact that 'the Negro slave immigrant of modern North America has been subject to the twofold penalisation of racial discrimination and legal servitude'.[744]

Pause, re-read, and carefully peruse upon the aforementioned paragraph again. The U.S. President Lincoln's political achievement concerning the abolition of slavery in the United States of America is in the socio-economic context of a black African-descent Negro human slave reduced to a tradeable commodity on the world economic market. A living and breathing commodity, deprived of personal liberty and human dignity, a black African slave who

---

744 Toynbee, Arnold J. (1987). *A Study of History: Abridgement of Volumes I–VI.* New York: Oxford University Press, p. 128.

was not afforded equal protection under the law, a black slave that can be bought and sold; a black slave, not a free human, one that is regularly lynched, beaten to death, whipped, tortured, a black slave whose biological children are the rightful and lawful property of the white male Christian American slave owner, in which the early modern U.S. legal framework afforded no constitutional protection or human rights to the black African Negro slaves.

Yes, it is in this aforementioned context, that the U.S. President Lincoln went against the social-political-legal-economic establishment, and dominant proslavery U.S. public opinion to abolish slavery in the United States of America. In fact, the U.S. President Lincoln created a definitive national anti-slavery norm in the U.S. with his *Proclamation of Emancipation 1863*. The U.S. President Lincoln's God-given human conscience did not permit the immoral institution of slavery to endure any longer in the United States of America.

In concise terms, what the U.S. President Lincoln did was transform the political dynamics of a *'fight for the abolition of slavery'* into a *'fight for the territorial integrity of the Perpetual Union'* to psychologically motivate the U.S. white male Christian population to proceed to civil war for the abolition of slavery in the quest to save the Perpetual Union of the United States of America. It is self-evident that President Lincoln did not remain satisfied with the precarious and delicate political balance of *The Missouri Compromise of 1820*, one that aimed to preserve the balance of power between the 'free' states and the 'slave' states within the American Union, a political agreement that prohibited slavery North of the latitude of 36°30′. In Lincoln's own words, the U.S. President's iron resolve to unite the United States of America, and irreversibly destroy the immoral and unjust institution of slavery is vividly expressed herein, 'I expect to maintain this contest until successful, or till I die'.[745]

---

745 McPherson, James. (2003). *Battle Cry of Freedom: The Civil War Era*. New York: Oxford University Press, p. 555.

The *Missouri Compromise* itself was a short-lived political settlement and represented a finite and fractious compromise between the pro-slavery and anti-slavery states that ultimately faltered with the *Kansas-Nebraska Act 1854*. An act of the U.S. Congress that permitted the free people of Kansas and Nebraska to legally determine for themselves whether to permit or outlaw slavery within their respective state's territory.

In retrospect, it was the formidable leadership of the U.S. President Lincoln that fundamentally and decisively altered the national trajectory of the United States of America on the matter of slavery. An alteration of trajectory of the national conscience that terminally led to the disintegration of slavery in the United States of America. U.S. President Lincoln's political rhetoric positioned into motion the free white Catholic Irish man, to die for the freedom of the unequal black African Negro slave. Few political leaders can fundamentally re-calibrate the *vox populi* (voice of the people) for such moral ends that promote the egalitarian ideals of eternal law and social justice on the Earth. The U.S. President Lincoln is one of the greatest political statesmen in the last millennium of international political history; 'such a man might be a copy to these younger times'.[746]

Ultimately, despite the death, destruction, and devastation that was caused during the *U.S. Civil War* (1861–1865), the evocative lyrics of the aspirational *Battle Hymn of the Republic* that was sung across the North American continent, were secured by the just and moral cause of the Perpetual Union:

> 'As ye deal with My contemners,
> so with you My grace with you shall deal;
> Let the Hero, born of woman, crush the serpent with His heel,
> Since God is marching on.

---

746 Shakespeare, William. (1623). *All's Well That Ends Well*. Act 1, Scene 3.

CHAPTER 6 | HISTORY AND JURISPRUDENCE

> *He has sounded forth the trumpet that shall never call retreat:*
> *He is sifting out the hearts of men before His judgment seat:*
> *Oh, be swift, my soul, to answer Him! Be jubilant my feet!*
> *Our God is marching on!*
>
> *In the beauty of the lilies Christ was born across the sea,*
> *With a glory in His bosom that transfigures you and me;*
> *As He died to make men holy, let us die to make men free'.*[747]

In 1963, one hundred years later, in the United States of America, this had become the universal and mainstream societal perception—that the black African Negro slaves were now free people, no longer reducible to human slaves, not beneath the universal value of human dignity. The social, political, and economic focus had now shifted to the African American's Civil Rights Movement (1954-1968), which demanded equal constitutional and legal rights for African American's in the United States of America.[748] The most prominent amongst the African American civil rights advocates being Martin Luther King, Jr. (1929-1968) who is revered for his prominent '*I Have a Dream*' speech that was delivered in Washington D.C. in 1963 (see Figure 46). This was a profound speech that galvanised the American people, the U.S. government, and the American political leaders into decisive action.

Now let us momentarily digress from the primary discourse on slavery, to consider the historical atrocities, social injustice, economic oppression, and legal disparity for women throughout the annals of human history due to the operation of institutionalised *patriarchy*. A fundamental and radical shift in the role of women in the Western civilisation significantly began to garner momentum in

---

747 Howe, Julia Ward. (1863). *Battle Hymn of the Republic*. Philadelphia: Supervisory Committee for Recruiting Colored Regiments. U.S. Library of Congress. Date accessed: 22 May 2020. Access link: <https://www.loc.gov/resource/rbpe.33700100/>
748 Prominent figures of the U.S. Civil Rights Movement included: Martin Luther King Jr., Rosa Parks, Malcolm X, and John Lewis.

Figure 46: The Reverend Dr. Martin Luther King, Jr.
Image Credit: American Photo Archive / Alamy.

the nineteenth century. As an example, consider the unprecedented example of Elizabeth Blackwell (1821–1910), who was the first British born female physician to earn a Medical Degree from the Geneva Medical College (New York City) in 1849.[749] Thereafter, Elizabeth Blackwell was also the first women to be listed on the British General Medical Council's Medical Register.

In addition, it is only over the course of the last two centuries, that women obtained the legal right to vote in the modern civilised world, with New Zealand granting women the legal right to vote in 1893 (see Figure 47). Thereafter, followed by Denmark granting women universal suffrage in 1915, Russia also provided women with the legal right to vote in 1917, and the United States of America followed suit in 1920 with the *Nineteenth Amendment* to the U.S. Constitution. Historically, within the United States of America, to

---

[749] In 1821, in the United States of America, women had no access to higher education or the established professions, and married women had no legal identities separate from their husbands.

CHAPTER 6 | HISTORY AND JURISPRUDENCE

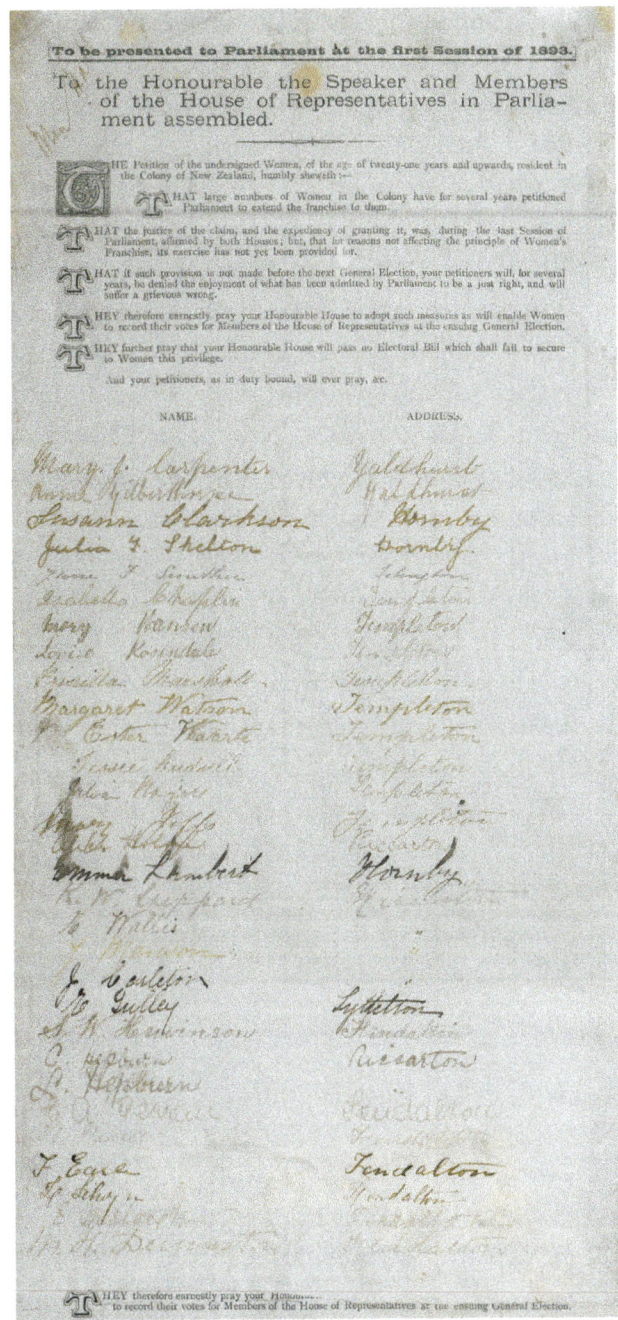

Figure 47: Women's Suffrage Petition to the New Zealand Parliament.
Image Credit: Archives New Zealand [Item No. LE1 1893/7a].

be eligible to vote, one had to be male, white, and an owner of real property. There was an exception to the criterion on the ownership of real property, for the Anglo-Saxon and European descent men that had served in the United States Army.

The progressive, democratic, liberal, secular, and modern Western contemporary history is full with examples of institutionalised legal discrimination against women in the conventional human society. For example, consider that the Holy Bible (NIV) in *Ephesians at 5:22* which explicitly states: 'Wives, submit yourselves to your own husbands as you do to the Lord', or the statement at *Ephesians 5:24*, 'Now as the Church submits to Christ, so also wives should submit to their husbands in everything'. As a further example, consider in the case of modern France, the *French Civil Code of 1804*, Article 213 which asserted, 'a husband owes protection to his wife, a wife, *obedience* to her husband', this article was legally in force in France until 1938.[750]

Alternatively, let us briefly examine the civilised and enlightened British civilisation's treatment of women in the Anglo-Saxon modern conventional society. In 1840, a British judge *authorised a husband to beat his wife and to hold her prisoner* so long as he did so 'without cruelty'.[751] It was only in 1878, that the British Parliament passed an act permitting English women to petition the English law courts for separation on the 'grounds of assault'.[752] In addition, in 1893, a British statute extended this legal right to women to

---

750 Arnaud-Duc, N. Chapter 4: The Law's Contradictions in: Friasse, G., and Perrot, M. (1993). *A History of Women in the West. Volume IV: Emerging Feminism from Revolution to World War.* Cambridge: Massachusetts: Harvard University Press, p. 98.
751 F. Basch. (1837). *La Femme en Angleterre de l' avenement de Victoria (1837) a la Premiere Guerre mondiale in: Histoire mondiale de la femme.* Paris: Nouvelle Librairie de France. 1966, Volume 4, p. 199.
752 Arnaud-Duc, N. Chapter 4: The Law's Contradictions in: Friasse, G., and Perrot, M. (1993). *A History of Women in the West. Volume IV: Emerging Feminism from Revolution to World War.* Cambridge: Massachusetts: Harvard University Press, p. 99.

include 'persistent cruelty' as grounds for a lawful divorce from their husband (or, historically, Lord).[753]

Universally, social customs, cultural traditions, and established social norms serve to reinforce the status quo and determine the behaviour and psychology of people and their role (i.e., position, class, and status) in the modern civilised society. As an example, consider the classic case of the Chinese civilisation's antiquity cultural practice of foot-binding for women in the conventional Chinese society.[754] Alternatively, investigate the contemporary example of the Padaung women in Northern Thailand, who wear brass neck rings as a cultural symbol of their ethereal beauty.[755]

In addition, the U.S. is not without its own moral transgressions against natural law and natural justice concerning the position and status of women in the Anglo-American society. In 1873 the U.S. Supreme Court heard the infamous *Bradwell v Illinois* case, and the highest appellate Court of the land, inequitably, improperly, and unjustly, upheld the distinction of sex in the modern American civil society; the gender bias precedent, that it was the unparalleled and exclusive purview of men to practice law ... 'the paramount destiny and mission of women is to fulfil the noble and benign offices of wife and mother'.[756] These aforementioned examples represent only a handful of select cases throughout the human civilisation that demonstrate the institutionalised injustices and inequalities that women confronted in the modern conventional society, solely on the basis of their sex.

---

753   Arnaud-Duc, N. Chapter 4: The Law's Contradictions in: Friasse, G., and Perrot, M. (1993). *A History of Women in the West. Volume IV: Emerging Feminism from Revolution to World War.* Cambridge: Massachusetts: Harvard University Press, p. 99.
754   See: Ko, Dorothy. (2005). *Cinderella's Sisters: A Revisionist History of Footbinding.* First Edition. California: University of California Press Books.
755   Theurer, Jessica. (2014). Trapped in Their Own Rings: Padaung Women and Their Fight for Traditional Freedom. *International Journal of Gender and Women's Studies.* (December 2014), Volume 2, No. 4, pp. 51–67.
756   United States Supreme Court. (1872). *Bradwell v State of Illinois.*

The gender-based discrimination that women confront in the modern conventional society is entirely unjust and deplorable. How is it an equitable and just state of affairs within the modern society when a person is judged on the basis of one's sex, and this serves as the determining or crucial factor for one's ability to receive a quality formal education, enter a distinguished and reputable profession, earn a personal income, and further develop one's mental and intellectual faculties, and achieve success in the modern civilised world? Not to mention, that a human possesses no demonstrable control over their sex, as genetically determined by the 'X' and 'Y' chromosomes. One should be judged on character, morals, intentions, actions, and merit, not on the basis of sex, race, religion, colour, ethnicity, social class, gender, private wealth, fame, education, income, fortune, reputation, or some other discriminatory biological, social, economic, legal, or political factor.

Universally and historically, women have been kept economically dependent upon men in the human society, denied their civil, political, and legal rights, denied equal representation to participate in all dimensions of the conventional human society, and denied fair and equal remuneration for professional work women performed in the conventional society—solely on the grounds of their sex.[757] Sex discrimination has, and albeit to a lesser degree and extent, continues to be practiced in the twenty-first century within the sovereign nation-states across the modern civilised world. In the United States of America, the *Civil Rights Act 1964* legally barred discrimination in employment on the basis of sex. In Australia, the *Sex Discrimination Act of 1984* had the same intended effect, however, employment equality and economic parity between men and women in the contemporary modern civilised society are far

---

[757] Australian Human Rights Commission. (2018). *Face the Facts: Gender equality 2018*. Australian Human Rights Commission. Date accessed: 5 February 2018. Access link: <https://www.humanrights.gov.au/education/face-facts/face-facts-gender-equality-2018>

from realised in both the United States of America, and in the Commonwealth of Australia.

In respect to the global advocacy movement of *feminism*; women's rights to be equal to that of men in the modern civilised society; an ideology that was once considered extreme, unacceptable, and an anomaly to the public function of the conventional society— namely the exercise of legal, political, civil, and economic rights of women, in the twenty-first century is considered mainstream, and accepted as an axiomatic truth. However, the forces of history, law, religion, society, language, culture, and politics have all ensured an enduring legacy upon the inequality that women continue to confront in the twenty-first century modern civilised society.

The outdated ideation of women representing the *Sexus Sequior* (the second sex) has entrenched sexual inequality (also known as gender inequality) in the modern society. This ingrained (or institutionalised) sex distinction positions a unique role for 'affirmative action' to promote greater gender equality within the modern sovereign nation-states and the contemporary modern civilised world.

972

On global human population growth. According to the United Nations, the projected growth trajectory in the world human population from the year 2000 to the year 2100 is from 5.3 billion to 11.2 billion, respectively.[758] This United Nations forecast represents an unprecedented significant human population growth in any 100-year period in the entire world history of the human civilisation.[759]

---

758 United Nations Department of Economic and Social Affairs. (2017). *World Population Prospects: Key findings and advance tables. 2017 Revision.* Working Paper No. ESA/P/WP/248. United Nations Department of Economic and Social Affairs: Population Division. Date accessed: 20 February 2020. Access link: <https://population.un.org/wpp/Publications/Files/WPP2017_KeyFindings.pdf>

759 United Nations Department of Economic and Social Affairs. (2019). *Global*

For the human species sexual desire is insatiable. For the male's spermatozoa and the women's fertile ovarian follicles which produce ova, seek the life force of the will-to-live, a phenomenon beyond the control of humanity, when coupled with the human's dominion over nature that has rendered nature's natural destructive forces (i.e., famines, flash floods, bushfires, earthquakes, pandemics, hurricanes, epidemics, tornadoes, volcanic eruptions, cyclones, and tsunamis) less pertinent to a significant degree, if not redundant, in relation to the human existential survival capacity on the Earth. Nonetheless, the modern scientific, mechanical, medical, artificial intelligence, robotic, and the information and communications technological advancements of the human civilisation will inevitably result in unprecedented and unsustainable excesses in the global quantum of the human population on the Earth.

This forecasted unprecedented growth in the human population only further serves the ambitions and endeavours of the aristocratic and capitalist's elite class. The affluent social class for whom the additional poor children born from the booming global human population translate into future human capital. The destitute and unlettered working class will sell their productive human labour power surplus for the furtherance of the private wealth creation and preservation of those ultra-high net worth individuals at the very top stratum of the societal hierarchy and neoliberal economic world order. The aforementioned scenario is the newfound conventional reality; the epitome of modernism, individualism, industrialism, capitalism, materialism, urbanism, industrialism, neoliberalism, consumerism, secularism, atheism, liberalism, and globalism in the contemporary modern civilised world.

Issues: Population. United Nations Department of Economic and Social Affairs. Date accessed: 28 July 2019. Access link: <https://www.un.org/en/sections/issues-depth/population/>

CHAPTER 6 | HISTORY AND JURISPRUDENCE

973

Based on the documented human history of war and conflict, from its earliest written records created by Herodotus (ca. 484 BC – 425 BC) in *The Histories*, humans will be well advised to keep a Lilliputian quantity of hope in humanity to converge as a unified and singular human civilisation. A human civilisation that is peace-loving and demonstrates the superior capacity to engage in mediation, conciliation, arbitration, negotiation, and diplomacy, to resolve all transgressions, threats, breaches of the peace, tirades, and disagreements in the modern civilised world is a distant dream. Rather, the outbreak of world war and armed conflict, not to mention, constant attempts by sovereign nation-state's and independent non-state actors to undermine the fragile safeguard of international peace and security throughout the four corners of the Earth is more likely than not the true conventional reality.

The conditions for a 'perpetual peace' on the Earth will forever remain beyond the reach of the human civilisation, as demonstrated by over two and a half millennia of recorded human history; from the *Peloponnesian War* (431 BC – 404 BC) to the *Syrian Civil War* (2011–Present).[760] Regrettably, war and conflict are the permanent attributes of the human existential condition within the realm of this physical world. Whereas diplomacy and peace represent the temporary conditions in the conventional modern civilised world.

In the context of the condition of belligerency between two or more hostile sovereign nation-states within the international relations of the modern civilised world, a decisive military victory by one belligerent nation-state only serves to establish the causal grounds for an unfavourable political solution. That is the imposition of an unjust peace treaty, on the basis of the unconditional surrender of the defeated and conquered nation-state.[761] Consequently, the

---

760 Kant, Immanuel. (Ted Humphrey, Trans.) (1983). *Perpetual Peace and Other Essays*. Indianapolis: Hackett Publishing, p. 23.
761 Julius Caesar. (ca. 100 BC – ca. 44 BC). 'War gives the right to the conquerors

Victor's Justice that ensues only serves to ensure that peacetime then becomes the founding basis for the preparation of a future war by the defeated and conquered nation-state.[762] And so, the vicious cycle of the '*Thucydides Trap*' continues in perpetuity within the conventional reality, until the extinction of one of the belligerent civilisations.[763] The following rational observation of the Athenian historian Thucydides is universally applicable in the affairs of international relations, regardless of the particular two variables concerning the 'established power' and the 'rising power', '… the growth of Athens' power and Sparta's fear was, in my view, the cause which compelled them to go to war'.[764]

974

On the written record of the orthodox and documented historical record of the human civilisation. History is not what it is purported to be. For it is *not the actual events that have transpired* that come to define human history, nor is the historical record categorically independent of human and natural events. Yet, it is *the subjective and partial interpretation and systematic recording of such events*, which when catalogued in a particular and distinct method, come to project a pre-established notion of how the history of the human species in the physical world is recorded and perceived.

---

to impose any condition they please upon the vanquished.' See: Jr. Freeman, Chas. W. (1993). *The Diplomat's Dictionary*. Washington D.C.: National Defence University Press, p. 393.

762   'The greatest crimes which afflict society are all committed under the false pretence of justice. The greatest of all crimes, at least that which is the most destructive, and consequently the most opposite to the design of nature, is war; but there never was an aggressor who did not gloss over his guilt with the pretext of justice.' See: G.W.B. (1940). *The Best Known Works of Voltaire*. London: Harper & Brothers, p. 456.

763   Allison, Graham T. (2017). *Destined for War: Can America and China escape Thucydides's Trap?* New York: Houghton Mifflin Harcourt, p. 362.

764   Roberts, J. M., and Westad, O. A. (2013). *The History of the World*. Sixth Edition. New York: Oxford University Press, p. 196.

CHAPTER 6 | HISTORY AND JURISPRUDENCE

The inquisitive reader is directed to inquire more fully into the historical fact that Polydore Vergil's *Anglica Historia* (1534) was written under the royal auspices of His Majesty King Henry VII (r. 1485–1509), to legitimise Henry VII's forceful seizure of the English throne and the Crown of England from His Majesty King Richard III (r. 1483–1485), the latter King of England and Lord of Ireland whom was defeated by Henry VII's military forces at the Battle of Bosworth Field in 1485.

As an in-depth example of the aforementioned philosophical assertion, we shall consider the significant political events of the twentieth-century in the modern People's Republic of China (est. 1949). For example, consider *The Great Leap Forward* (1958–1962), and *The Great Proletarian Cultural Revolution* (1966–1976). Two major public policy catastrophes of the People's Republic of China's Founding Chairman Mao Zedong (r. 1949–1976). The former state policy directive contributed to the *Great Chinese Famine* (1958–1961), which is estimated to have resulted in 'forty-two to forty-three million deaths according to an official fact-finding mission conducted in the early 1980s', not accounting for the deaths of Chinese civilians due to torture and state incarceration by the Chinese Communist Party.[765] The latter communist nation-state policy led to the degradation and demise of China's ancient history, art, literature, churches, shrines, libraries, and much of its obligatory culture and feudal traditions since antiquity. Not to mention, the eradication of the intelligentsia, all of which collectively served to position the late twentieth century trajectory of the Chinese sovereign nation-state towards that of a regressive wayward and third-world sovereign nation-state. Ultimately, at the apex of the Cultural Revolution, Chairman Mao's Red Guards were tasked with

---

765 See: Dikotter, Frank. (2010). *Mao's Great Famine: The History of China's Most Devastating Catastrophe, 1958–1962*. Great Britain: Bloomsbury Publishing, p. 333.
Jisheng, Yang. (2013). *Tombstone: The Great Chinese Famine, 1958–1962*. New York: Farrar, Straus & Giroux, p. x, and 197.

the national agenda to destroy 'The Four Old's—Old Ideas, Old Customs, Old Habits of mind, and Old Culture' of the pre-modern Chinese civilisation.[766]

However, China's Chairman Mao Zedong (1893–1976) continues to be remembered in modern China as a revered revolutionary political figure, one who expunged the Japanese occupation, not to mention, eliminated European imperialism, conquest, domination, and empire from the sovereign territory of China. Chairman Mao is respected as a nationalist founding father of modern China that eradicated the Western civilisation's modern exploitation of China and the foreign Western nations application of the European legal fictitious *Doctrine of Extraterritoriality*; as part of the 'unequal treaties' enforced upon China during its self-proclaimed 'Century of Humiliation'.[767, 768] For example, consider the legally binding *Treaty of Nanjing* (1842) entered into between the High Contracting Parties of Great Britain and China.

In addition, historically, Chairman Mao Zedong is perceived as a liberating figure and politically unifying figure of modern China. Mao was a Chinese revolutionary leader who transcended the aforementioned hostile foreign forces operating in the People's Republic of China during the nineteenth and early twentieth centuries, to bring political stability, social harmony, and economic equality to the Chinese people.[769] Thus, Mao's Red Army's arduous *Long March*

---

766 Muhlhahn, Klaus. (2019). *Making China Modern: From the Great Qing to Xi Jinping*. Cambridge: Harvard University Press, p. 466.
767 Wang, Dong. (2003). The Discourse of Unequal Treaties in Modern China. *Pacific Affairs*. Volume 76, No. 3, Fall, 2003, p. 399.
768 Harris, Richard. (1959). China and the World. *International Affairs*. Volume 35, No.2, April 1959, p. 162.
769 *The Boxer Rebellion* (1899–1901), which resulted in the Allied Victory and enforcement of the *Boxer Protocol* in 1901. *The Eight-Nation Alliance* sent their troops into combat in China in response to the Boxer Rebellion. *The First Opium War* (1839–1842) and *the Second Opium War* (1856–1860), which resulted in a British victory, and the subsequent territory of Hong Kong being ceded to the United Kingdom from 1841 to 1997. Prior to 1841, Hong Kong has effectively been a part of China for over 2,000 years, since its incorporation into China during the Qin dynasty in 243 BCE. In addition, Macau was a former colony of

CHAPTER 6 | HISTORY AND JURISPRUDENCE

(1934–1935) was after all not in vain, for the hostile foreign forces that fabricated and created the causal ground conditions for political rebellion and civil discord amongst the Chinese population in the nineteenth and early twentieth centuries were finally defeated and expelled from mainland China. Not to mention, the foreign Western forces that supported the Nationalist Kuomintang Army, were to be conclusively defeated by the revolutionary and nationalist leader Mao Zedong.

Nonetheless, the *Long March* of 1934–1935 is an impressive military achievement by Mao's Red Army, for previous Chinese attempts at ousting such foreign hostile influences had thus far proven unsuccessful. A prominent example being, during the reign of the *Qing Dynasty* (1644–1912), the Chinese people staged an infamous uprising. Namely, the *Boxer Rebellion 1899* which was aimed at the eradication of foreign Christian, British, Japanese, Russian, and the broader Western influences in modern China. In response, an international military force was established to supress the nationalist uprising and was victorious in defeating the Chinese Boxer nationalists (see Figure 48).[770]

Notwithstanding, the historical accuracy and validity of the excesses and gross abuses of foreign nation-states upon modern China, one shall pause to ruminate and reflect, that Chairman Mao's actions and government policies killed four times as many civilians as Hitler's radical and fundamental NAZI political ideology that purged ca. 6 to 8 million Jewish people from Germany and the wider European continent during the reign of the *Third Reich* (1933–1945). In fact, Chairman Mao's political policies killed twice as many Chinese civilians, more specifically, ca. 45 million Chinese dead, compared to the atrocities committed by the Imperial Japanese

---

the Portuguese Empire from 1557 until 1887, when Portugal was given perpetual colonial rights to Macau, the foreign colonial rule came to an end in 1999.

770   The international force consisted of approximately 20,000 troops from eight nations (i.e., Austria-Hungary, France, Germany, Italy, Japan, Russia, the United Kingdom, and the United States of America).

Figure 48: Chinese Boxer Rebellions executed upon their defeat by foreign belligerent nation-states.
Image Credit: The Wellcome Library (London) [Item No. 663487i].

Army in China.[771] The Imperial Japanese Army during its twentieth-century imperial conquest and ruthless domination of China; was responsible for approximately 14–20 million Chinese deaths, during the course of the *Sino-Japanese War* (1937–1945), and the greater Japanese merciless and oppressive colonial occupation of modern China.[772]

A universal political lesson to be deduced herein is that regardless whether it be the particular twentieth century cases of Hitler, Mao, Lenin, Gaddafi, Hussein, Kim Il-sung, Stalin, Idi Amin, or Pol Pot, the dismal conventional political reality, as noted by

---

771 Dikotter, Frank. (2010). *Mao's Great Famine: The History of China's Most Devastating Catastrophe, 1958–1962.* New York: Bloomsbury Publishing, p. 333.
772 Mitter, Rana. (2013). *China's War with Japan, 1937–1945: The Struggle for Survival.* London: Allen Lane, p. 6.

CHAPTER 6 | HISTORY AND JURISPRUDENCE

Sri Lanka's (and the modern civilised world's) first female Prime Minister Sirimavo Bandaranaike, is that 'history is full of examples of the disastrous consequences that came upon such nations that changed their constitutions by giving one man too much power'.[773]

Ultimately, the human history subjectively records and assigns importance to political and humanitarian crisis, from a biased, partial, and value-laden perspective, that treats human life and sovereign nation-states with inequality. As an example, consider that it is an established twentieth century fact the NAZI Holocaust resulted in at least six million Jewish people being massacred during the *Third Reich*, however, in comparison, human history scantly affords much remembrance and acknowledgement of the Soviet Union's *Holodomor* (see Figure 49), which, according to one estimate, claimed the lives of at least five million Ukrainian civilians.[774] Alternatively, consider the twentieth century *Armenian Genocide* which was sanctioned by the 34th Sultan of the Ottoman Empire Abdul Hamid II (r. 1876–1909), during the declining and terminal phase of the Ottoman Empire, which resulted in the deaths of between 664,000–1,200,000 Armenian Christians.[775]

Not to mention, that seldom and scant historical attention has been afforded to the Imperial British Empire's engineered atrocities of *The Great Bengal Famine* (1770) in British India, which witnessed the deaths of approximately 10,000,000 Indian people across the South-Asian subcontinent during the British East India Company's extraterritorial dominion over India from 1757–1858. The Great

---

773 Asian Human Rights Commission. (2010). *Sri Lanka: An appeal made to all members of parliament of Sri Lanka by a group of Sri Lankan citizens to vote against the 18th Amendment to the Constitution.* Asian Human Rights Commission. Date accessed: 20 February 2020. Access link: <http://www.humanrights.asia/news/forwarded-news/AHRC-FST-068-2010/>
774 Conquest, Robert. (1986). *The Harvest of Sorrow.* New York: Oxford University Press, p. 306.
775 U.S. Holocaust Memorial Museum. (2019). *The Armenian Genocide (1915–16): In Depth. Holocaust Encyclopedia.* Date accessed: 16 December 2019. Access link: <https://encyclopedia.ushmm.org/content/en/article/the-armenian-genocide-1915-16-in-depth>

Figure 49: Malnourished Russian children during the Russian famine, 1921–1923.
Image Credit: International Committee of the Red Cross Archives / S.N. / Russia, 1922 / Malnourished Russian children during the Russian famine, 1921–1923 / Item Reference: V-P-HIST-01312-21.

Bengal Famine of 1770 was excessively deadly, in terms of human casualties, and in numerical comparison, it amounts to ca. 25 per cent of the 40,000,000-death toll from *World War 1* (1914–1918). However, this British atrocity is barely mentioned as a footnote in the modern Western history of the human civilisation, and it does not constitute an outlier either, of the immoral British civilisations dishonourable and impressive record of war crimes and colonial oppression of the coloured people of the modern civilised world.

For the history of the human civilisation repeated itself yet again, with *The Bengal Famine* of 1943. This latter famine occurred during the period of direct British Raj over India (1858–1947), and the then British Prime Minister Winston Churchill's racist imperial policies and colonial political determinations which resulted in the preventable deaths of ca. 3,000,000 Indian people.[776] Indeed, the British government employed the systematic political and economic instrument of induced famines in foreign nation-states, in order to ensure that the foreign and hostile national populations remained subservient to the British Empire's global interests. This was an act of British foreign policy to ensure that the foreign and alien civilisations and colonial territories remained in total servitude to the sovereign British Crown. Even for the unlettered human, it is not overly difficult to deduce parallels between the British engineered famines in modern India and the *Irish Potato Famine* (1845–1849) in Ireland. Lest we forget.

In addition, let us consider the historical case of the United States of America, post the *Spanish-American War* of 1898, which resulted in a decisive U.S. military victory and the settlement of the *Treaty of Paris* (1898). The Treaty of Paris permitted the United States' annexation and incorporation of the foreign territories of Guam (1898) and Hawaii (an incorporated territory from 1898–1959, until Hawaii was admitted as the 50th state into the Perpetual Union in 1959).

In addition, consider the persistent U.S. illegal military occupation of the sovereign Cuban territory—Guantánamo Bay (1898–Present)—which the U.S. considers its protectorate territory.[777] Not to lessen the historical recognition of the U.S. former imperial and colonial occupation of the Philippines (1898–1946), the U.S. lease of Diego Garcia (1966–Present), which is strategically located in the British Indian Ocean Territory (BIOT), and the legal status of Puerto Rico as an unincorporated territory of the United States of America (1898–Present).

---

776 Mishra, Vimal., Tiwari, Amar Deep., Aadhar, Saran., Shah, Reepal., Xiao, Mu., Pai, D.S., and Lettenmaier, Dennis. (2019). Drought and Famine in India, 1870-2016. *Geophysical Research Letters*. Volume 46, No. 4, (28 February 2019), pp. 2075-2083.

777 According to the *Platt Amendment (1903)*; a treaty between the U.S. and Cuba, the United States maintains and governs the Guantanamo Bay Naval Base and the Guantanamo Bay detention camp located in Cuban territory.

Such amoral and reprehensible imperial conduct by the U.S. sovereign and independent nation-state, in direct violation of the international law; a nation-state which is supposedly founded upon the idealistic, moral, and democratic principles enshrined within its founding document; the *U.S. Declaration of Independence* (1776), such reprehensible and inexcusable belligerent conduct seems wholly permissible to it.[778]

However, Imperial Japan's annexation of Korea in accordance with *The Japan-Korea Treaty* of 1910 is regarded as an act of aggression; a war crime against the Korean people, in the orthodox record of the modern history. Not to mention, the Imperial Japanese Army's rape of women during *World War II* (1939–1945) is a war crime against humanity. The U.S. systematically tarnished the reputation of the Japanese civilisation with political propaganda in the early decades of the twentieth century.

Yet when the U.S. Armed Forces engaged in the *Vietnam War* (1955–1975), they killed civilians, burned property, and raped Vietnamese women, in particular, as evidenced by the *My Lai Massacre* (1968). This inhumane war-time conduct was an atrocity that the American Armed Forces repeated; having engaged in similar dishonourable military conduct previously against the North Korean people during the armed conflict of the *Korean War* (1950–1953). Apparently, perhaps most conveniently, there are not many widely published and transparent (unretracted and declassified) official U.S. government documents in the public domain, that establish the credible and authentic historical narrative of the U.S. Armed Forces unconscionable military conduct during the Korean and Vietnamese Wars in our contemporary historical records to

---

778 'We hold these truths to be self-evident, that all men are created equal, that they are endowed by their Creator with certain unalienable Rights, that among these are Life, Liberty, and the Pursuit of Happiness.' See: U.S. National Archives. (2019). *United States Declaration of Independence (1776)*. U.S. National Archives. Date accessed: 8 September 2019. Access link: <https://www.archives.gov/founding-docs/declaration-transcript>

peruse on this subject matter that specifically castigates the United States of America.

In addition, consider the British war crimes against humanity in the *First Boer War* (1880–1881), and the *Second Boer War* (1899–1902), with the British civilisation being the pioneer of 'concentration camps'. However, the British Government's contribution to the starvation and torture of political prisoners is seldom discussed in the field of international human rights abuses. Not to mention, the British Government's flagrant violation of the international humanitarian law in the nineteenth and twentieth centuries.

The orthodox modern historical record scantly affords remembrance to the British Empire's imprisonment of Indian political activists and nationalist and pro-independence movement leaders. As an example, consider that in the twentieth century, Mohandas Karamchand Gandhi (1869–1948) (see Figure 50), who was arrested on the charge of sedition by the British officials in Bombay, India, for protesting against the colonial rule of the British Raj in India (1922). However, in the midst of colonial oppression and despair, Gandhi never lost hope for a Free India, 'When I despair, I remember that all through history the ways of truth and love have always won. There have been tyrants, and murderers, and for a time they can seem invincible, but in the end, they always fall'.[779]

In addition, Jawaharlal Nehru (1889–1964), the head of the Indian Congress, was also arrested by the British authorities and sent to prison, following the *Quit India Resolution* passed by the Indian Congress Party (1942). In the grand scheme of world history, what did the British civilisation proffer to the modern civilised world? The British Crown, the British Commonwealth, Colonialism, the Corporation, and the Concentration Camp.

---

779   Youth for Human Rights International. (2020). *Champions of Human Rights: Mahatma Gandhi (1869-1948)*. Youth for Human Rights International. Date accessed: 13 March 2021. Access link: <https://www.youthforhumanrights.org/voices-for-human-rights/champions/mahatma-gandhi.html>

Figure 50: British educated Indian lawyer and anti-colonial nationalist Mahatma Gandhi.
Image Credit: Science History Images / Alamy.

However, in the modern Western world, we are constantly reminded and reinforced of the more contemporary human rights abuses of the Middle Eastern and African countries (i.e., Libya under the political leadership of Muammar al-Gaddafi (r. 1969–2011) in the early twenty-first century modern civilised world). Such is the political situation that these oppressed and exploited poor third-world sovereign nation-states require the *'Responsibility to Protect'* (R2P) Doctrine to be institutionalised as the modern *Ius Gentium* (Law of Nations) by the United Nations Security Council. Why? In order that the 'International Community' of the civilised modern sovereign nation-states, shall thereafter, possess the requisite legal means; the force of the international law to intervene in the internal affairs of the third-world sovereign nation-states. For the purposes of permitting an international humanitarian intervention, presumably aimed at safeguarding the civilian population of a sovereign nation-state, when its own sovereign (i.e., head of state) cannot unconditionally guarantee the same desired political objective.

Where was this 'International Community', not when 223 civilians were reportedly killed in Libya in the 2011, but when ca. 800,000 innocent civilians died in the *Rwandan Genocide* of 1994?[780, 781] Alternatively, where was the 'solidarity' of the 'International Community' when ca. 2,000,000 African people died as a result of war and famine during the *Biafra Genocide* (1967–1970); a genocide that was effectuated during the *Nigerian Civil War* (1967–1970)?[782] Rather, the International Community was

---

780 'In eastern Libya, where the uprising began as a mix of peaceful and violent protests, Human Rights Watch documented only 233 deaths in the first days of the fighting'. See: Kuperman, A. J. (2015). *Obama's Libya Debacle: How a Well-Meaning Intervention Ended in Failure.* Foreign Affairs. March/April 2015 Edition.

781 BBC News. (2019). *Rwanda genocide: 100 days of slaughter.* BBC News. Date accessed: 11 May 2020. Access link: <https://www.bbc.com/news/world-africa-26875506>

782 Combat Genocide Association. (2020). *Biafra 1966–1970.* Combat Genocide Association. Date accessed: 11 May 2020. Access link: <https://combatgenocide.org/?page_id=90> For a detailed analysis see: Korieh, Chima J. (2012). *The*

polarised into two distinct factions; with the pro-Nigerian state group consisting of Great Britain, East Germany, Egypt, and the Soviet Union, whilst the pro-Biafra group that was in favour of the Biafra state secessionist movement and consisted of China, France, Ireland, and Israel.

Meanwhile, the U.S. officially declared 'neutrality' in relation to the Biafra-Nigerian armed conflict, with the U.S. Presidential Candidate Nixon asserting on 9 September 1968: 'Until now, efforts to relieve the Biafra people have been thwarted by the desire of the central government of Nigeria to pursue total and unconditional victory, and by the fear of the Ibo people that surrender means wholesale atrocities and genocide. But genocide is what is taking place right now—and starvation is the grim reaper'. [783]

By stark contrast, the contemporary political history of Libya illustrates that in 2011, prior to the U.S. led military intervention force, Libya had the 'Highest Human Development Index, the lowest infant mortality, and the highest life expectancy in all of Africa'. [784] Post the U.S. humanitarian intervention, Libya has become a failed nation-state. Libya is an Arab nation-state that is now a safe haven for terrorist groups, characterised by lawlessness, and effectively governed by the political ideology of violent and radical anarchism. The overarching theme of this stanza is that one should inquire into the accuracy of recorded historical observations for oneself, and diligently endeavour to undertake a more comprehensive and universal analysis of world history, in order to be able to analyse historical realities in a more objective, impartial, and complete manner.

Nigeria-Biafra War: Genocide and the Politics of Memory. New York: Cambria Press.
783 Olawoyin, J. A. O. (1971). *Historical Analysis of Nigerian-Biafra Conflict.* Thesis (LL.M.) York University, pp. 137–139.
784 Zaman, Asad. (2018). *The Business of War.* Medium. Date accessed: 14 December 2019. Access link: <https://medium.com/@asadzaman_27/the-business-of-war-995af1355594>

975

Positive laws enacted by the elected representatives of the people within a sovereign nation-state, and the unelected professional, expert, technical, and specialised bureaucrats within the international institutions, and the inter-governmental organisations, that participate in the processes governing the enactment of international law, primarily function to minimise war and conflict in the modern civilised world. However, the secular institution of law cannot eliminate world war and conflict, just as it cannot unconditionally guarantee international peace and security in the modern civilised world.

976

In the contemporary modern civilised world, in so far as the *Ius Commune* (Common Law) is concerned, and notwithstanding human morality, which may indeed stand on higher ground, and be operable to the contrary, one's relational concern for a fellow human does not extend beyond the legal 'Duty of Care' in the human society. As long as this duty is met, discharged, satisfied, and extinguished, legally, to the minimum extent required by the institution of positive law, one's concern and regard for another human is fulfilled.

For one can competently meet the minimum requirements of the *'Duty of Care'* legal doctrine that is established by positive law, and see to it that in the notable absence of the exercise of one's moral conscience, that in its place, one demonstrates a calculated, contractual, commoditised, commercial, and conditional interest; a disposable monetary interest that does not extend beyond the individual equitable profit interest or underlying economic motive towards another human in the conventional society.

For the defining moral litmus test of compassion and benevolence, that is governed and operable by the natural and moral law of human conscience, is always the more stringent factor in the determination of how humans ought to conduct themselves and their interactions with other constituents of the human society, rather than the legal 'Duty of Care' doctrine that is operable at common law in the modern civilised society.

977

In the contemporary modern civilised society, women may exercise considerable and significant autonomy over the selection of the male sex partner, whose spermatozoon is to impregnate their ovum, excluding the immoral and criminal acts of non-consensual copulation, sexual assault, and rape.

However, this philosophical assertion does not extend to the female's ability to exercise legal jurisdiction over the determination to proceed with, or terminate, her immediate pregnancy at any point from the initial phase of conception (the formation of a single-cell embryo—zygote), up to the final phase of the human pregnancy, being immediately prior to the live birth of a neonate. It is established that the commencement of the female's conception begins once the ovum has been fertilised by the male's spermatozoon in the ampulla of the fallopian tube and the resulting synergy (the union of gametes) has created the zygote cell.

For once the fertilised ovum has commenced prenatal development in the uterus, and when the human embryo, in the near future, is due for a live birth through the *pudendum,* or a caesarean section birth, then predominantly the male sex, that is to infer men who are elected as ministers of the sovereign parliament, with parliamentary privilege, legislate through statutes and acts of parliament, the days and weeks at which the female sex may repudiate her pregnancy. That is to infer it is the lettered and affluent men who come to legislate and legally determine when a woman can seek an abortion, or be lawfully compelled to continue with the pregnancy until the fetus is born.

CHAPTER 6 | HISTORY AND JURISPRUDENCE

Now if it is not lettered and affluent men within sovereign parliaments, then the alternative recourse, which is corresponding in number and value, that is namely confronting predominantly male judges in a court of law, or an appellate court, in the modern civilised society that come to exercise the legal and judicial force to determine outcomes that impact women in relation to their abortion rights. Is this not repugnant conduct in a civilised, democratic, modern, liberal, and secular sovereign Western nation-state? Objectionable conduct demonstrated by the advanced and progressive Western civilisation that presumably exhibits the hallmarks of equality, freedom, dignity, and liberty of its people.

Given that the conceived human life; the fetus, is within the female's inviolable body, is she not the true sovereign of the fetus? Must the impregnated female sex not be given the ultimate and final legal, moral, and ethical authority, the requisite personal autonomy, to determine what is to eventuate with respect to the fetus contained within the confines of her physical body? Now acknowledging that the development of parliamentary legislation and judge-made case law that constitutes the modern *corpus juris* (the body of common law) is to the contrary and determined overwhelmingly by lettered, aristocratic, privileged, and affluent men in the modern civilised society, then what innate freedom does the ordinary female embody to lawfully exercise her own free-will, autonomy, agency, conscience, self-determination, and judgement in respect to the continuation, completion, or termination of her pregnancy?

In the contemporary modern civilised society, the female sex cannot even come to determine one of the most fundamental medical decisions concerning her immediate human life—to terminate the dependent and unborn phenomenon of life within her inviolable human body. Historian's Kathy Peiss and Christina Simmons accurately portray the nuances of the socio-economic inequality and legal discrimination towards the female sex by asserting that 'Sexuality is not an unchanging biological reality or a universal natural force, but rather, a product of political, social, economic, and cultural process, that is to infer, sexuality has a history' to its development and evolutionary trajectory in the human society.[785] Perhaps, in a particular sense, it can be argued that 'one is not born, but rather becomes, a woman' by the institutionalised gender stereotypes, psychological conditioning, sexualisation, socialisation, and domestication of women to give birth to children and observantly or dutifully fulfil the benign role of house wife or domestic servant in the traditional and pre-modern human society.[786]

In addition, the reader is strongly encouraged to examine the conventional personification of female gender roles in the modern civilised society. Not to mention, the lack of 'equal employment opportunity' and no 'equal pay for equal work' afforded to women in the modern civilised world. This is institutionalised sex discriminiation which only serves to demean the socio-economic status, and degrade the position of women in the contemporary human society.[787]

Now to return to the primary discouse on abortion rights, the female's individual right to an abortion is as much a moral, philosophical, theological, religious, and ethical question, as it is a legal, technological, medical, and scientific one, however, why is the female sex that it most effects marginalised? Why is the female's human right to affirm or deny the phenomenon of life being legislated and adjudicated predominantly by men (the opposite sex)?

Given that men have no immediate, nor proximate, practical life experience and immediate understanding of childbirth; for then the male sex is not the fittest and competent sex to enact medical

---

785   Peiss K., and Simmons C. 'Passion and Power: An Introduction' in: Peiss. K., Simmons C., and Padgug, R. A. (Eds.) (1989). *Passion and Power: Sexuality in History*. Philadelphia: Temple University Press, p. 3.
786   de Beauvoir, Simone. (1973). *The Second Sex*. New York: Vintage Books, p. 301.
787   According to the Australian Government 'Workplace Gender Equality Agency', in Australia the base salary gender pay gap was 15.5 per cent between men and women for the 2018–19 financial year. See: Workplace Gender Equality Agency. (2018). *The gender pay gap*. Workplace Gender Equality Agency. Date accessed: 18 December 2020. Access link: <https://www.wgea.gov.au/topics/the-gender-pay-gap>

practice guidelines, case law, or legislative determinations over this human life concerning moral quandary. Thus, it is improper for learned men to pass legal judgement and create legislation over ethical, moral, medical, and sexual issues of which they are not even the primary stakeholder, to the greater detriment, marginalisation, and exclusion of women in the contemporary modern civilised society.

978

On War and Conflict. War and conflict have been part and parcel of human existence as evidenced throughout the history of the human civilisation. History is destined to repeat itself. As select examples, consider the following, albeit finite, yet illustrative and demonstrable record of international conflict known throughout the annals of the human civilisation:

- The Peloponnesian War (431 BC – 404 BC)
- The First Punic War (264 BC – 241 BC)
- The Second Punic War (218 BC – 201 BC)
- The Third Punic War (149 BC – 146 BC)
- The First Crusade (1096–1099)
- The Second Crusade (1145–1149)
- The Third Crusade (1189–1192)
- The Fourth Crusade (1202–1204)
- The Fifth Crusade (1217–1221)
- The Sixth Crusade (1228–1229)
- The Seventh Crusade (1248–1254)
- The Eighth Crusade (1270)
- The Ninth Crusade (1271–1272)
- The Hundred Years' War (1337–1453)
- Austrian-Hungarian War (1477–1488)
- The First Siege of Vienna (1529)
- The Eighty Years War (1568–1648)

- The Thirty Years War (1618–1648)
- The Second Siege of Vienna (1683)
- The Seven Years War (1756–1763)
- The First Boer War (1880–1881)
- The Second Boer War (1899–1902)
- World War I (1914–1918)
- World War II (1939–1945)
- The Korean War (1950–1953)
- The Vietnam War (1955–1975)
- The Lebanese Civil War (1975–1990)
- The Iran-Iraq War (1980–1988)
- The Afghanistan War (2001–2021)
- The Iraq War (2003–2011)
- The Syrian War (2011–Present)

The aforementioned cases of armed conflict are by no means representative of an exhaustive or comprehensive list of all the human conflicts since time immemorial. However, what these wars collectively come to define is the consistency with which war and conflict takes precedence and prevails over international peace and security throughout the annals of the human civilisation.

The aforementioned dismal universal record of war and conflict is most illustrative of the universal phenomenon of the will-to-live; the will's embodiment of an endless and purposeless desire to dominate and secure power as an outward expression, as a manifestation, of its inner irrational, destructive, blind, and chaotic instinct, within the phenomenal world. The 'will to power' is the ultimate tangible expression of the will in action, in its futile attempt to secure the imposition and manifestation of its internal desires, universally upon the physical world.[788] In fact, this unceasing, purposeless, irrational, and relentless insatiable drive of

---

788 Nietzsche, Friedrich. (Walter Kaufmann, and R. J. Hollingdale, Trans.) (1968). *The Will to Power*. Random House, p. 148.

the will has come to determine and define human actions within the phenomenal world since time immemorial.

This universal belligerent conduct is further vested and reflected in the artificial socio-economic constructs and political-legal institutions with the applicable fictitious legal doctrine of *'International Legal Personality'*. In praxis this operable international law doctrine extends to sovereign and independent nation-states, international institutions, inter-governmental organisations, multinational corporations, monarchs, and churches. Institutions, agencies, corporations, associations, and entities that are ultimately led by human actors who assume high office, and hold public or private positions of privileged office within the conventional civil society's economic, legal, social, religious, medical, and political entities in the modern civilised world.

Ultimately, it is the human actors within the public and private spheres of the conventional society, whom discharge power across the social, legal, political, medical, religious, and economic institutions; federal government, sovereign parliaments, law courts, hospitals, the royal office, medieval churches, the papacy, the independent nation-state's armed forces, and so forth, *ad infinitum*, as a direct, immediate, and proximate consequence of the manifestation of the universal phenomenon of the will-to-live.

In the final analysis, humans can never co-exist in a world of *'Perpetual Peace'* so long as the human civilisation populates the Earth.[789] This is Immanuel Kant's logical fallacy, his idealistic and fanciful normative philosophy, one that fails to incorporate the dismal conventional reality of the phenomenal world. An impractical Kantian philosophy that incorrectly attempts to render obsolete and invalid both the ancient and modern history of the human civilisation in excess of four millennia.

---

789   Kant, Immanuel. (Ted Humphrey, Trans.) (1983). *Perpetual Peace and Other Essays*. Indianapolis: Hackett Publishing, p. 23.

979

There are two major components to the history of the human civilisation:

1. The creation and production of history
2. The transmission and record of history.

The two aforementioned components of history are quite distinct. For it is one aspect of history; the outcomes, the externalities, and the social realities, that arise out of the human production of history itself. And yet it is a second (subsequent) aspect; in relation to those people in positions of power in the human society, that find it favourable to exercise their prestigious and influential capacity (i.e., scholars, university professors, deans, reputable authors, chancellors, teachers, researchers, writers, and historians), to determine, and to record human history in such a subjective and partial manner that they best perceive proper and advantageous, in the best possible light, to achieve their desired ends and intended purposes more likely than not in accordance with—victor's justice of the victorious nation-state! The recorded history of the human civilisation is never distant from biased human interpretation and subjective analysis.

980

Humans do not learn from the dismal record of history; they do not heed its practical and invaluable lessons as demonstrated by the events of the *Peloponnesian War* (431 BC to 404 BC). The International Relations of the Greco-Roman world of antiquity, that established the political concept of a *Thucydides' Trap*, which arose from a culminating series of military battles between Sparta (a rising power, supported by the Persian Empire), and Athens (an established power), contains several invaluable historical lessons for the human civilisation.⁷⁹⁰ Regrettably, these are the historical lessons which humans, time and time again, fail to heed, including in the contemporary modern civilised world.

In the ancient world's history, during the Golden Age of Greece, Sparta and Athens amalgamated their armed forces to collectively defeat the colossal Persian Empire in the *Greco-Persian Wars* (499 BC to 449 BC), only to subsequently, succumb to the fundamental forces of human nature, that is to consequently fight each other in the *Peloponnesian War* (431 BC to 404 BC), with Sparta reigning victorious.

Despite the passage of *The Middle Ages, The Age of Discovery,* and *The Age of Enlightenment*, the ancient and modern history of the political, military, economic, and diplomatic dimensions of International Relations remain immensely similar in their most fundamental and basic tenets. This fixed conventional reality is demonstrated by the example of Imperial Japan and the United States of America, in the nineteenth century and into the twentieth century. In the nineteenth century, both sovereign nation-states were friendly states, however, in the twentieth century, both states became bitter adversaries and went to war in *World War II* (1939–1945), with the U.S. reigning victorious, and consequently imposing a military occupation upon the conquered and defeated Japan (1945–1952).

The moral proposition of this stanza is that political alliances and enemies periodically change like the contours of sand dunes. At a particular period in time, natural persons or artificial entities can converge upon the same side, however, at a later period in time, the two allies can become divergent to one another's initial positions.

---

790 This term was coined by the Harvard University Professor Graham Allison to capture the idea that the rivalry between an established power and a rising one often ends in war. See: Allison, Graham. (2012). *Thucydides's trap has been sprung in the Pacific*. Financial Times. Edition of 22 August 2012. Date accessed: 29 July 2019. Access link: <https://www.ft.com/content/5d695b5a-ead3-11e1-984b-00144feab49a>

Herein, the *Holy Alliance 1815* is a classic example of the monarchist great powers of Austria, Prussia, and Russia forming a political coalition to restrain the ideological opposing and contending forces of liberalism, republicanism, and secularism, that sought to displace the established and institutionalised order of feudalism and monarchism in the aftermath of the destruction caused by Napoleon Bonaparte (1769–1821) in the *French Revolutionary Wars* (1792–1802).

However, half a century later, two of the three members of the Holy Alliance of 1815; Austria and Prussia, went to war with each other in the *Austro-Prussian War* of 1866.[791] Ultimately, all of the human history is an eternal and repetitive struggle characteristic of universal war and conflict. That is an irrational and perpetual struggle for the supremacy of unassailable power and total political domination by one distinct ethnic-racial civilisation on the Earth.

981

Führer Adolf Hitler (r. 1933–1945) was categorically correct about one universal human observation within the physical world; that all of the significant history of the human civilisation concerns war and conflict between one distinct racial-ethnic group of the human civilisation and another.[792] This categorical assertion is evidenced as far back as the ancient Egyptian civilisations' enslavement of the Hebrew people in ancient Egypt.

The human existential reality for eternity is as *The Holy Bible* has inscribed; 'What has been will be again, what has been done will be done again; and there is nothing new under the Sun.'[793] All of the human civilisations' history, that has been, presently is, and will be written, shall be characteristic of the domination of one ethnic-

---

[791] Also known as *the Seven Weeks War (1866)*.
[792] Hitler, Adolf. (Michael Ford, Trans.) (2009). *Mein Kampf: The New Ford Translation*. California: Elite Minds Inc., p. 115.
[793] The Holy Bible. (New International Version). *Ecclesiastes 1:9*.

racial group of the human civilisation against the oppression of another ethnic-racial group of the human civilisation. This eternal process of perpetual conflict and irrational struggle leads to the unique state of peace, prosperity, and progress for the 'free' races of the human civilisation, and in stark contrast, death, disease, and destruction for the 'oppressed' races of the human civilisation.

The aforementioned inhumane political situation is almost identical in the twenty-first century Anglo-American world order, as it was approximately four hundred years antecedent in the Anglo-Saxon world order. As an example, consider that in the seventeenth and eighteenth centuries on the North American continent, the white British, Irish, and Scottish foreign settlers; the white Anglo-American's who suppressed and subjugated the black African Negro slaves in the Thirteen U.S. Colonies, now in the twenty-first century treat the emancipated black African American slaves inhumanely and with extreme cruelty, in direct violation of the Eighth Amendment to the U.S. Constitution which explicitly prohibits 'cruel and unusual punishments'. [794]

Nonetheless, the free black African American people are still subjugated and treated like second-class citizens of the United States of America. For example, consider the treatment of the African American Donald Neely, who was arrested by the Galveston Police Force in 2019 and led through the streets of the city tied to a rope with officers on horseback in Texas, the United States of America.

It is self-evident that the long-term societal effects of the racial segregation and disenfranchisement policies that were institutionalised by the *Jim Crow Laws* in the United States of America have not been wholly overcome in the early twenty-first

---

794   Campbell, James S. (1964). Revival of the Eighth Amendment: Development of Cruel-Punishment Doctrine by the Supreme Court. *Stanford Law Review*. Volume 16, No. 4, (July 1964), pp. 996–1015.
Heffernan, D. (1996). America the Cruel and Unusual? An Analysis of the Eighth Amendment Under International Law. *Catholic University Law Review*. Volume 45, Issue 2, (Winter 1996), Article 5, pp. 481–560.

century American society. In fact, it can be argued that the free black African American is still treated like a black Negro slave in the twenty-first century United States of America. For example, consider the 2020 murder of George Floyd in police custody by Minneapolis Police Officer Derek Chauvin in the state of Minnesota, the United States of America. As long as the universal absence of natural justice, social equality, natural law, and moral law fail to prevail across the entire human civilisation, there shall never arise a durable and eternal peace on the Earth. *Pacem in terris* (Peace on Earth) is not possible.

The Law of Nations is a fictional legal concept; the conventional reality of International Relations is determined by the *Realpolitik* of power; conquer or be conquered, after all International Politics is the 'art of the possible'.[795] In the final analysis, there exist but two categories in which all the people of the human civilisation can be positioned; the *Free* people, and the *Oppressed* people.

982

History is not necessarily a true and accurate representation of the important events that have transpired within the physical world. *How* the significant events that have been transcribed in the recorded history of the human civilisation are remembered, and *what* actually transpired are two distinct matters.

Those who create the physical world in their distinct image, through victory, secured by the instruments of military force, genocide, famine, nuclear weapons, slavery, depopulation, violence, and forced population displacement, necessary elements in a state of belligerency, come to possess the requisite and vested agency to subsequently record the world's history as they judge proper and fit.

---

795 Sturmer, Michael. (1971). Bismarck in Perspective. *Central European History.* Published by: Cambridge University Press on behalf of Central European History Society. Volume 4, No. 4, 1870/ 71, (December 1971), p. 318.

CHAPTER 6 | HISTORY AND JURISPRUDENCE

That is, to record their endeavours and legacy in a favourable light—*Victores Iustitia* (the Victor's Justice).

983

Regressive, backward, and wayward cultures and civilisations inevitably capitulate to foreign and progressive cultures, leaders, institutions, practices, ideas, and religions. As an example, consider the *Islamisation* of Brunei, Egypt, India, Indonesia, Malaysia, Philippines, Singapore, Turkey, and by extension, the newly created modern sovereign nation-states of Bangladesh, Mali, Pakistan, and Sudan. In addition, as an example, consider the *Christianisation* of African, Asian, and Middle Eastern sovereign nation-states in the modern era, such as Angola, Burundi, Cape Verde, Congo, China, Cyprus, Ethiopia, Ghana, India, Kenya, Lebanon, Malawi, Namibia, Rwanda, South Korea, South Sudan, Uganda, Zambia, and Zimbabwe.

Last but not least, as an additional example, consider the *permanent British and European colonial settlement* of the newfound world; the Commonwealth of Australia, the Dominion of Canada, New Zealand, and the United States of America. These significant events of the modern international political history are demonstrable of the fact that the backward, uncivilised, and Indigenous people, the traditional civilisations, and the ancient cultures were unable to resist the innovative, liberal, democratic, modern, industrial, scientific, and technological prowess of the progressive British and European civilisations. The fundamental premise of this stanza is that the physical world is subject to constant change—adapt, or perish and become a relic of the world's history!

In the modern international political context, dominated by the Western civilisation, there exists one, and only one anomaly in the modern world history—Imperial Japan. It is a remarkable achievement that the culture, language, institutions, identity, religions, and history of the Japanese civilisation, have remained predominantly intact since antiquity, despite the transformative modernisation, privatisation, urbanisation, Anglicisation, Westernisation, Christianisation, Europeanisation, Islamisation, colonisation, Sovietisation, industrialisation, and globalisation within the International Relations of the modern civilised world over the last four centuries.

Despite the modern Anglo-Saxon and Anglo-American world order, modern Japan has predominantly been able to preserve and keep intact its distinct culture, history, customs, traditions, social norms, and language. Not to mention, Japan was an exclusive non-European sovereign nation-state to possess its own imperial empire and foreign territories (i.e., Formosa, Korea, Kuril Islands, Manchuria, and Shandong) in the modern era predominantly characterised by American, British, and European colonialism, mercantilism, and imperialism.

The Empire of Great Japan (1868–1947); a Far East Empire in Asia that for a brief period of the twentieth century, made Anglo-Saxon white Christian men into slaves, and had them carry the yellow Shinto man's burden during *World War II* (1939–1945). This is an unprecedented first and only reversal, let alone unorthodox creation, of the modern world history of the human civilisation in the distinct image of the Japanese civilisation. Lest we forget, that Imperial Japan's achievements were secured during a period in modern history, in which the Western civilisation was the dominant political, economic, social, legal, military, industrial, scientific, and technological force in the modern civilised world.

A modern world where it was long established and accepted that the black men of the African civilisation were born to be slaves, and the inferior Asian civilisation of colour were unfit for self-rule, unfit for self-determination, unfit for self-government, and most unfit for the grand political endeavour of civilian government of their colonised nation-states by the Great European Colonial Powers (i.e., Belgium, Great Britain, Denmark, France, Germany,

Italy, the Netherlands, Portugal, Spain, Sweden, and the United States of America) of the modern civilised world.

Furthermore, despite Japan's surrender and defeat in *World War II* (1939–1945), Japan's success in the post-*World War II* international order has been nothing short of truly remarkable. The interested and inquisitive reader ought to investigate the successful Japanese penetration of international markets with its *Keiretsu's* and *Zaibatsu's*. Notable examples of successful Japanese conglomerates include; Akai, Canon Inc, Casio Computer Co. Ltd, Citizen Watch Co. Ltd, Dai-Ichi Kangyo Bank Ltd, Daikin Industries Ltd, Epson, Fujifilm Holdings Corporation, Fujitsu Ltd, Fuji Xerox Co. Ltd, Honda Motor Company Ltd, Isuzu Motors Ltd, Japan Victor Company (JVC), Kawasaki Heavy Industries, Komatsu Limited, Mazda Motor Corporation, Minase, Mitsubishi Motors, Mitsui Bank, NEC Corporation, Nikon Corporation, Nissan Motor Co Ltd, Orient Watch, Panasonic Corporation, Sanyo Electric Co. Ltd, Seiko Holdings Corporation, Sharp Corporation, Sony Corporation, Subaru Corporation, Suzuki Motor Corporation, Taiyo Kobe Bank, Toshiba Corporation, Toyota Motor Corporation, and Yamaha Corporation.

984

Why should we, the people, accept the imposition of the positive laws of a sovereign and independent nation-state which oppresses and suppresses its people?[796] *Lex iniusta non est lex* (An unjust law is no law at all)![797]

985

The progression of the human civilisation, from the natural and primitive environment of the hunter-gatherer society, to the agrarian society, to the contemporary artificial industrialised, urbanised, secularised, privatised, globalised, and modernised environment of the human society; from the most primitive hunting and

---

[796] '... the voice of the whole people would be thus fairly, fully, and peaceably expressed, discussed and decided by the common reason of the society. if this avenue be shut to the call of sufferance it will make itself heard thro' that of force, and we shall go on, as other nations are doing, in the endless circle of oppression, rebellion, reformation; and oppression, rebellion, reformation again, and so on forever.' Jefferson, Thomas (1743–1826). See: U.S. National Archives. (1816). Proposals to Revise the Virginia Constitution: 1. Thomas Jefferson to 'Henry Tompkinson' (Samuel Kercheval), 12 July 1816. The Jefferson Papers. U.S. National Archives. Date accessed: 12 September 2019. Access link: <https://founders.archives.gov/documents/Jefferson/03-10-02-0128-0002> [Original source: *The Papers of Thomas Jefferson*, Retirement Series. Volume. 10, *May 1816 to 18 January 1817*. Edited by: J. Jefferson Looney. Princeton: Princeton University Press, 2013, pp. 222–228.]
'One has a moral responsibility to disobey unjust laws.' See: King Jr, Martin Luther. (1963). *Letter from Letter from Birmingham Jail* in Rieder, Jonathan. (2014). *Gospel of Freedom: Martin Luther King, Jr.'s Letter from Birmingham Jail and the Struggle That Changed a Nation*. New York: Bloomsbury Press, p. 174.
'An unjust law is itself a species of violence. Arrest for its breach is more so.' See: Gandhi, Mahatma. (1948). *Non-violence in Peace and War*. Ahmedabad: Navajivan Publishing House, p. 150.
'Unjust laws exist; shall we be content to obey them? Or shall we endeavor to amend them and obey them until we have succeeded? Or shall we transgress them at once?' See: Thoreau, Henry D. (Philip Smith, Ed.) (1993). *Civil Disobedience and Other Essays*. New York: Dover Publications, p. 7.

[797] Saint Augustine. (Peter King, Ed.) (2010). *Augustine: On the Free Choice of the Will, On Grace and Free Choice, and Other Writings*. New York: Cambridge University Press, p. 10, and 122.

gathering, ancient, and rural human society to the progressive, civilised, urbanised, Westernised, and the most scientifically and technologically advanced state of the contemporary modern civilised society, has resulted in the displacement of those humans who have failed to adapt to the new modern civilised world.

For change creates both opportunity and inequality, and the incumbents who represent the 'status quo' are disadvantaged, and the innovative pioneers proceed to make favourable gains, given the social consequences of their enacted changes within the re-orientation of the conventional human society.

986

The origins of contemporary modern positive law and political order reside within the antecedent violence and suppression of the human society. A *revolution* that has achieved its primary objectives, and has now become enshrined and static in the political organisation and socio-economic function of that particular human society. Those individuals who demonstrate resistance, need to be transcended or subdued; otherwise, a *counter-revolution* remains a plausible future reactionary outcome within the sovereign body politic.

987

There exists no public order without law enforcement.

988

The Western civilisation's modern emancipation of human rights was a struggle that ensued over the course of eight centuries from 1215 to 2006; with some significant outcomes including:

- *The English Magna Carter 1215*
- *The Petition of Right 1628*

- *The English Bill of Rights 1689*
- *The Declaration of the Rights of the Man and of the Citizen 1789*
- *The United States Bill of Rights 1789*
- *The Geneva Convention for the Amelioration of the Wounded in Time of War 1864*
- *The Geneva Convention for the Amelioration of the Condition of the Wounded and Sick in Armies in the Field 1906*
- *The Geneva Convention Relative to the Treatment of Prisoners of War 1929*
- *The Universal Declaration of Human Rights 1948*
- *The Geneva Convention Relative to the Protection of Civilian Persons in Time of War 1949*
- *The European Convention on Human Rights 1950*
- *The Convention Relating to the Status of Refugees 1951*
- *The International Convention on the Elimination of All Forms of Racial Discrimination 1965*
- *The International Covenant on Civil and Political Rights 1966*
- *The International Covenant on Economic, Social, and Cultural Rights 1966*
- *The Convention on the Elimination of All Forms of Discrimination Against Women 1979*
- *The United Nations Convention Against Torture 1984*
- *The Convention on the Rights of the Child 1989*
- *The Rome Statute of the International Criminal Court 1998*
- *The International Convention for the Protection of All Persons from Enforced Disappearance 2006*

989

The modern human is a *homo sapien* who has been civilised, cultured, cultivated, conditioned, domesticated, educated, indoctrinated, socialised, medicated, and tamed. That is to say, the human has been reduced in the whole potential of its *human* existence to exclusively derive, or procure, an economic profit from one's particular actions and activities in the modern civilised society. For let us fundamentally question what it is, and what it precisely means to be 'Westernised', 'Anglicised', 'modernised' and 'civilised'? It is to communicate in the English language, be dressed in a modern corporate suit and formal business attire, eat fine foods with stainless steel cutlery, be an economically productive unit of human labour power, be Christianised, believe in Jesus of Nazareth as your Saviour, follow Western, predominantly Anglo-American and Anglo-Saxon legal conventions, positive laws, social customs, and cultural traditions.

The modern civilised world is one that is very much founded on the Judeo-Christian tradition, laws, values, morals, dogmas, social norms, customs, religion, calendar, academic disciplines, date and time conventions, and etiquette practices. For if you do not socialise and conform within the pre-defined and prescribed criterion of being Westernised, Anglicised, modernised, and civilised, then, in the alternative, you are considered to be uncivilised, alien, inferior, an outlaw, a foreigner, barbaric, and backward—yet to become civilised.

As an in-depth example, let us consider the British civilisation's modern founding, colonisation, and settlement of the Australian continent. In 1770, the aforementioned scenario (i.e., one of the uncivilised, backward, foreign, and alien race of the Aboriginal people) is what Lieutenant James Cook (1728–1779) reasoned and concluded, upon his arrival on the newfoundland barrens of *Terra Australis Incognita* (the Unknown Southern Land), declaring the Australian continent to be *Terra Nullius* (Nobody's Land). Subsequently, in 1778, the formal founding of Australia, as a British Penal Colony, was established with Captain Arthur Phillip's (1738–1814) arrival at Sydney Cove, New South Wales on 26 January 1788. With the First Fleet anchored on the eastern shores of Australia (see Figure 51), the permanent British settlement of the Anglo-Saxon civilisation had now begun to take hold forthwith with the invasion, genocide, slavery, depopulation, and colonisation of the Aboriginal and Torres Strait Islander people in Australia.[798]

Figure 51: The foundation of the modern British Commonwealth of Australia by Captain Arthur Phillip at Sydney Cove, 1788.
Image Credit: The Royal Geographical Society / Getty Images.

Even though Indigenous Aboriginal and Torres Strait Islander people had lived on the Australian territory for over 60,000 years antecedent to European contact and the continents modern discovery by the British civilisation, notwithstanding, the Anglo-Saxon civilisation did not recognise, nor acknowledge, the Indigenous Australian and Torres Strait Islander civilisations to be the rightful and lawful traditional owners of the country by virtue

---

798 *The Draught Instructions for Governor Phillip* is the first official communication concerning the occupation and settlement of Australia. It empowers Captain Arthur Phillip to establish the first British Colony in Australia and to make grants of land and issue regulations for the Colony.

CHAPTER 6 | HISTORY AND JURISPRUDENCE

of their possession, connection, heritage, history, language, kinship, and flag.⁷⁹⁹ The unquestionable fact of Indigenous custodianship of Australia was dismissed as a fable, and the fiction of the Anglo-Saxon Commonwealth of Australia was institutionalised in its place. The British Commonwealth of Australia was founded upon a fiction, the undeniable historical fiction of *Terra Nullius* (Nobody's Land).

In direct contravention of the uncontestable veracity of the Australian Indigenous history, Captain Arthur Phillip (1738–1814) presumably founded Australia on behalf of the British Crown, with the then His Majesty King George William Frederick (1738–1820), asserting the legal doctrine of *Terra Nullius* (Nobody's Land) to be true, valid, and operable within the territory of the newfound British Commonwealth of Australia.⁸⁰⁰

Did the Anglo-Saxon people, the British civilisation, forget their common heritage and creed; *consuetudo pro lege servatur* (custom is held as law)? Let it be known that it is forever true—*consuetudo vincit communem legem* (custom overrules the common law)! The seizure of Aboriginal and Torres Strait Islander people's sovereign country was *ultra vires* (beyond the powers) of the sovereign British Crown, that is to infer, it was an unlawful and immoral act, period.

Notwithstanding, the unlawful and unfounded application of the *Terra Nullius* (Nobody's Land) fictional legal doctrine in the modern Commonwealth of Australia, the Aboriginal and Torres Strait Islander people lived in harmony, and within the proper moral bounds of human relationships and societal structures. That is to infer, the Aboriginal people lived in accordance with the

---

799 Working with Indigenous Australians. (2017). *60,000+ years ago to 1788*. Working with Indigenous Australians. Date accessed: 9 April 2019. Access link: <http://www.workingwithIndigenousaustralians.info/content/History_2_60,000_years.html>

800 'There is no greater tyranny than that which is perpetrated under the shield of the law and in the name of justice.' See: Montesquieu, Charles de. (Cohler, Anne M., Miller, Basia Carolyn., and Stone, Harold Samuel., Eds.) (1989). *Montesquieu: The Spirit of the Laws*. Cambridge: Cambridge University Press, p. 309.

moral, traditional, and natural laws pertaining to the Indigenous Australian's civilisation.

The Aboriginal and Torres Strait Islander people never required the artificial societal constructs of a police force, jail, drugs, financial capital, law courts for prosecution, modern prescription medication, step-mum, step-father, gay and lesbian relationships, not to mention, the introduction of alcohol, European diseases, state reservations, medical sterilisation, state government protection boards, and Christianity. These are all in fact socially engineered, artificial, and modern structures of the foreign and alien Western civilisation in Indigenous Australia. Do you know why Aboriginal and Torres Strait Islander people did not require a written constitution, legislature, police force, law courts, armed forces, sovereign parliaments, jails, common law, and financial capital?

Plainly due to the fact that the ancient Aboriginal and Torres Strait Islander culture and civilisation, was one founded upon the moral tenets of social justice and natural law. The Aboriginal and Torres Strait Islander civilisations were not established upon the British civilisation's 'progressive' principles of greed, self-interest, profit motive, private property, private enterprise, real property, pecuniary gain, pleasure, personal wealth, empire, imperialism, capitalism, mercantilism, liberalism, colonialism, and human labour power exploitation.

The Aboriginal and Torres Strait Islander people did not require the traditional Anglosphere artificial societal constructs and institutions; the British Crown, the British Commonwealth, the British Concentration Camps, the Anglican Church, the British Monarchs, the English common law, the concept of a representative and responsible government, the Westminster system of government, the English law courts, and the sovereign parliament, to act as constraining forces upon the egotistical humans in the Anglo-Saxon conventional society, to regulate and govern the English person's pursuit of self-interest, pleasure, profit, pecuniary gain, personal

CHAPTER 6 | HISTORY AND JURISPRUDENCE

wealth, private enterprise, and private property in the sovereign body politic.

At a fundamental point in human interaction within the urbanised, industrialised, privatised, Anglicised, Westernised, and modernised civilised society, if each and every constituent was to pursue one's selfish, particular, and narrow self-interested agenda, the conventional human society would no doubt enter into a state of anarchy and conflict!

That is why, in the modern Western civilisation, founded upon the pursuit of liberty, the profit motive, pecuniary gain, private property, private enterprise, personal wealth, artificial happiness, the purposeless longevity of the modern civilised human life, and self-interest, that such constraining forces (i.e., public institutions, the armed forces, positive laws, the British Crown, courts of law, federal, state, and local civil governments, prisons, hospitals, federal and state parliaments, and the police force), become a necessary instrument to the proper function and vital organisation of the modern conventional society, that itself is founded upon the artificial principles of self-interest, pecuniary gain, private enterprise, private property, pleasure, and liberty, which know no ends in their insatiable pursuit.

In stark contrast, the Aboriginal Australian and Torres Strait Islander civilisations lived in a state of 'natural liberty', in true harmony with nature, in accordance with naturalism, yet the British 'foreign' system of the Anglo-Saxon civilisation, of the Western civilisation, was in a forceful, radical, genocidal, and involuntary method, supplanted onto the Aboriginal and Torres Strait Islander people and their sovereign country, for some reason to represent a more superior, advanced, modern, and progressive 'English' concept of the human civilisation.

However, the Aboriginal and Torres Strait Islander people were deemed uncivilised, illiterate, and backward, according to the standard of the white Christian British man; a standard which was alien, foreign, and detrimental to the very existence of the free black Aboriginal and Torres Strait Islander people in Australia. The Indigenous people of Australia were measured against an undeserving foreign standard, clearly alien to them and their traditional and time-honoured ways of living a meaningful life. Before the arrival of the British civilisation in Australia, the Indigenous Australian civilisation's way of life was in accordance with the principles of *ius naturale, lex naturalis* (natural law) in the territory of Australia.

The native Aboriginal and Torres Strait Islander people lived human life as intended by the institution of nature, with authentic and genuine human freedom in their immediate vicinity and possession, with human dignity, they had no requirement for a written constitution, codified legislation, high court, monarchs, acts and statutes of parliament, state and federal courts, the British Crown, the English system of common law, legislatures, sovereign parliaments, police force, national assemblies, armed forces, and civil governments, resulting in endless and contentious litigation.

Furthermore, the Indigenous Australian people had no need for mass conspicuous consumption and the endless insatiable quest to satisfy material human needs within the artificial and bureaucratic Anglo-Saxon modern society, with the sole aim of accumulating profits and private property through the lawful exploitation of human labour power. The conventional truth is that the black Indigenous Australian people were never confined, never enslaved to toil, beyond that which was deemed necessary for one's existential survival. Thus, the Indigenous Australian people possessed absolute human freedom; natural liberty, in the fundamental and real sense of the term.

Now in the alternate case of the white Christian Anglo-Saxon people, one has been domesticated, medicated, incarcerated, institutionalised, socialised, conditioned, tamed, and cultured, to toil and exert the exercise of one's finite labour power for the enduring benefit of one's capitalist master; the exercise of one's labour power that is most reflective of involuntary indenture and servitude in the modern conventional society. Philosophically, in so far as can be conventionally construed, the white Christian Anglo-Saxon man has, against one's will, been deprived of true natural liberty; a higher freedom outside the constraining forces of the artificial, conventional, modernised, and civilised society.

In addition, the Indigenous people of Australia did not engage in colonialism, imperialism, mercantilism, empire, and foreign conquest; the domination of foreign lands, the oppression of foreign people of distinct races, and the eradication of their unique cultures. The Aboriginal and Torres Strait Islander people lived within their native territory and means, and did not impose, nor seek to impose, their way of life, language, culture, religion, history, practices, laws, social norms, morals, codes, or values, upon another foreign ethnic-racial group of people of the greater human civilisation. Nor did the Aboriginal and Torres Strait Islander people largely exhibit the modern societal problems of the Western civilisation: domestic violence, crime, relative poverty, economic inequality, social-class divisions, ageing population, drug and alcohol abuse, suicide, gambling, obesity, modern medical conditions, non-communicable diseases, and psychological disorders.

The Australian Aboriginal and Torres Strait Islander civilisations functioned and exercised the physical human body as intended by nature. The Indigenous Australian people had no systematic societal concept of private ownership of real assets, personal wealth, profits, pecuniary gains, economic industrialisation, international trade and commerce, legal contracts and international treaties, private enterprise, and private property. In short, fictitious legal constructs that have created a myriad of vexations in the modern civilised society.

In the twenty-first century, the Aboriginal and Torres Strait Islander Australians, exist as the most disadvantaged people in their own native country, that was superdeded by a British Commonwealth sovereign nation-state that is now representative of the white Christian Anglo-Saxon man's foreign British legal, political, social, medical, and economic systems and institutions. That is a British system of state governance that is all but foreign to the Indigenous traditional way of life and the Indigenous civilisation, writ large. The Anglosphere has been forcefully supplanted upon the Aboriginal Australia. The Aboriginal Australian people have been deprived of their legal, political, civil, human, cultural, and economic rights, including the:

- self-determination of the First Nation's people
- self-government within the Indigenous country
- right to freely assemble and associate
- right to freedom of expression
- right to freedom of speech
- right to their vested lawful claim as sovereign against the entire territory of the Anglo-Saxon occupied territory of Australia [the Commonwealth of Australia was established with the introduction of the alien and foreign Anglo-Saxon civilisation upon the native Aboriginal land. Therefore, the British Commonwealth has been constructed on the occupied Indigenous territory, and shall endure as long as the application of the British Crown's fundamental legal, political, economic, medical, cultural, and social system of oppression of the Aboriginal Australian people shall last]
- independence of their nation-state
- recognition of *de facto* sovereignty of their Indigenous country

Ultimately, the Australian Aboriginal people have become dependent and oppressed people, who are now overwhelmingly dependent on the British Commonwealth government's public housing schemes, public school education, welfare allowances, alcohol (i.e., the white man's water), food, and child support. This is the deprived, dismal, and deplorable socio-economic context of the Australian Indigenous people being the most incarcerated ethnic race on the Earth.[801, 802] Lest we forget.

The British civilisation, upon its inception onto Australia, sure did provide a 'new found freedom' for the Aboriginal and Torres Strait Islander people—an 'English' freedom that has deprived the Indigenous population of their ancient way of life, personal identity, natural liberty, pre-modern history, cultural heritage, mother tongue language, family ties, kinship, ancient traditions, and customary laws. For 65,000 years there was no 'Aboriginal problem' in Australia, it was 'created' by the advent of the Anglo-Saxon civilisation over the last 232 years in the British Commonwealth of Australia. Lest we forget.

According to data from the Australian Bureau of Statistics (ABS) which was presented in a 2017 report compiled by PricewaterhouseCoopers (PwC) titled *Indigenous Incarceration: Unlock the facts*, the Indigenous Australian people are imprisoned at rates far greater than the non-Indigenous Australian people in the Commonwealth of Australia. For example, consider the following findings contained within the aforesaid PwC report:

- Indigenous men are imprisoned at 11 times the rate of the general male population in Australia.
- Indigenous women are imprisoned at 15 times the rate of the general female population in Australia.

---

801 Schwarz, Kirrily. (2017). *If we're all equal, why are there so many Indigenous people in prison*. The Boiling Frog. The Law Society of New South Wales. Date accessed: 9 April 2019. Access link: <https://boilingfrog.com.au/equal-many-Indigenous-people-prison/>

802 Source: Australian Bureau of Statistics, Productivity Commission. (2013). Estimates of Aboriginal and Torres Strait Islander Australians, June 2011. Canberra: ABS; ABS. (2016). Prisoners in Australia, 2016. Canberra: ABS; AIHW. (2017). Youth justice in Australia 2015–16. Table S75a: Young people in detention on an average day by sex and Indigenous status, states and territories, 2015–16. AIHW. Bulletin no. 139. Cat. No. AUS. 211. Canberra: AIHW. In: PwC Australia. (2017). *Indigenous incarceration: unlock the facts*. PwC's Indigenous Consulting, p. 4. Date accessed: 9 April 2019. Access link: <https://www.pwc.com.au/Indigenous-consulting/assets/Indigenous-incarceration-may17.pdf>

- Indigenous children are imprisoned at 25 times the rate of non-Indigenous children in Australia.[803]

The *'White Man's Burden'* was considerably great for the Indigenous people of Australia to bear, and unfortunately, most members of the Indigenous civilisation died by the incidental introduction of the modern European diseases.[804, 805] For the Indigenous Australian people were unable to adapt and resist the modern British medical diseases and infections as a consequence of the white Christian Anglo-Saxon man's lifestyle, and the underdeveloped immune system of the Aboriginal and Torres Strait Islander people was strained from the introduction of the English civilisation and its modern way of life.

Furthermore, the Aboriginal and Torres Strait Islander people that did manage to survive the introduction of the British and European diseases, then had to contend with *The Frontier Wars* (1788–1939). The Black man's spears against the White man's guns. Needless to infer, that the former belligerent was doomed to total failure, and the conflict was decisively settled in the favour of the latter belligerent, before the first battle had even commenced in modern Australia.

The Indigenous Australian people that survived the incidence of European diseases and British genocide were literally enslaved, confined to government reservations, and had their biological children removed by lawful force—the phenomenon of *The Stolen*

---

803   Source: Australian Bureau of Statistics. (2016). Corrective Services, Australia, June Quarter 2016. Canberra: Australian Bureau of Statistics; AIHW. 2017. Youth Justice in Australia 2015–2016. AIHW. Bulletin No. 139, Cat. No. AUS. 211. Canberra: AIHW. In: PwC Australia. (2017). *Indigenous Incarceration: Unlock the Facts*. PwC's Indigenous Consulting, p. 5. Date accessed: 9 April 2019. Access link: <https://www.pwc.com.au/Indigenous-consulting/assets/Indigenous-incarceration-may17.pdf>

804   Kipling, Rudyard. (1899). *The White Man's Burden: The United States and The Philippine Islands*. In: Kipling, Rudyard. (1940). *Rudyard Kipling's Verse: Definitive Edition*. New York: Doueblday & Company, Inc.

805   Tuberculosis, Smallpox, Measles, Chickenpox, Cholera, Whooping cough, and Influenza.

Generations (1910–1970)—under the command of the Australian Board and Protection of Aborigines.

The malicious purpose of this state sanctioned action was for the Aboriginal people to be assimilated, and for the intended purpose of breeding out, rendering extinct, the Australian Aboriginal civilisation through the enactment of legal statutes and lawful acts vis-à-vis the Commonwealth of Australia's Parliament.[806] The Aboriginal and Torres Strait Islander Australian people have been dispossessed of their native land and lost their traditional way of life, and over the former three centuries have been subjected to:

- The white Anglo-Saxon man's church
- The white Anglo-Saxon man's alcohol
- The white Anglo-Saxon man's working paradise
- The white Anglo-Saxon man's vote
- The white Anglo-Saxon man's guns
- The white Anglo-Saxon man's language
- The white Anglo-Saxon man's religion
- The white Anglo-Saxon man's society
- The white Anglo-Saxon man's common law
- The white Anglo-Saxon man's government
- The white Anglo-Saxon man's culture
- The white Anglo-Saxon man's state reservation
- The white Anglo-Saxon man's medicine
- The white Anglo-Saxon man's hospital
- The white Anglo-Saxon man's museum
- The white Anglo-Saxon man's prison
- The white Anglo-Saxon man's cemetery.

The ulterior Anglo-Saxon civilisations purpose of the *Stolen Generation* program was to utterly destroy the Indigenous civil-

---

806 See: The Hon Prime Minister Kevin Rudd. (2008). *Full transcript of P.M.'s speech*. The Australian. Date accessed: 9 April 2019. Access link: <https://www.theaustralian.com.au/news/nation/full-transcript-of-pms-speech/news-story/3143dac870aec0145901e575ae79cc3b>

isation's gene pool, so that they will no longer have a sufficient population to breed, to continue their existence as an independent, unique, and distinct Indigenous civilisation in the British Commonwealth of Australia.

The modern scientific logic here is straightforward. The Anglo-Saxon civilisation will undertake active measures (i.e., genocide, involuntary assimilation into the British culture, forced medical sterilisation, confinement onto state government reservations, institutionalisation into British schools, indoctrination into Christian churches and missionaries, teaching the English language, solitary confinement, the forced removal of Indigenous children from their families and integration into Anglo-Saxon families, institutionalisation of the Aboriginal children into orphanages and missionaries, incarceration of the Aboriginal population, the involuntary application of drugs and medication upon the Aboriginal population, and the unlawful enslavement of the Aboriginal people), all to eradicate the gene pool of the Aboriginal Australian population. When the gene pool of the Indigenous civilisation is severely reduced this shall inhibit in-group variation and diminish the variety of genes for fruitful human sexual reproduction, as genetic variation is essential to sustain the composition of this distinct Indigenous Australian ethnic-racial group of the human civilisation.[807]

As the Chief Medical Officer and the Protector of Aboriginal people for the Northern Territory, Dr. Cecil Cook (1897–1985), once stated, 'generally, by the fifth and invariably by the sixth generation, all native characteristics of the Australian Aborigine are eradicated. The problem of our half-castes will quickly be eliminated by the complete disappearance of the black race, and the swift submergence of their progeny in the white'.[808] In the twenty-first century modern

---

[807] Australian Human Rights Commission. (1997). *Report of the National Inquiry into the Separation of Aboriginal and Torres Strait Islander Children from Their Families*. Canberra: Commonwealth of Australia, p. 162.

[808] Australian Human Rights Commission. (1997). *Report of the National Inquiry into the Separation of Aboriginal and Torres Strait Islander Children from Their*

civilised society, rather than right the wrongs of the twentieth century; the Australian federal, state, and territory governments immoral practices that resulted in *The Stolen Generations*, the inequitable, discriminatory, and prejudiced policies against the Aboriginal people have largely remained in place in Australia.

The Anglo-Australian civilisation has now further emboldened and embarked upon repeating the traumatic and inhumane past atrocities of the twentieth century in the twenty-first century. As opposed to the historical practices of institutionalising the Aboriginal Australian child into the white Christian family foster care environment, or placement on the Christian missionaries, or confinement on the state government reserves, this time, the Indigenous Australian children as young as 10 years of age are being institutionalised in prisons and incarcerated in jails across the Commonwealth of Australia.[809] This is the creation of The Stolen Generation 2.0; this is the contemporary formation of 'The Incarcerated Generation' of Indigenous Australians.

One with a moral conscience, has to ask the following abstruse question. On what legal basis is a 10-year-old Indigenous Australian child, a minor, being sent to an Australian prison? As a modern civilised society, is it fair and just for a child to be institutionalised in prison, to be held fully responsible for their 'criminal' actions? Yet, of prime importance in this subject matter, one has to further inquire, why is an *Aboriginal child* under 10 years of age being sent to prison?

One must consider, what is to become of the future of a 10-year-old Indigenous Australian child, when that child is released from prison, and thereafter, enters adult life in the contemporary white Anglo-Saxon Australian society? Having spent a portion

---

Families. Canberra: Commonwealth of Australia, p. 118.

809 Human Rights Law Centre. (2019). *Stop putting kids in prison: Australian Governments told*. Human Rights Law Centre. Date accessed: 22 February 2020. Access link: <https://www.hrlc.org.au/news/2019/11/29/stop-putting-kids-in-prison-australian-governments-told>

of adolescent life in prison, most of these Indigenous Australian children are likely to take recourse in and be consigned to a life of alcohol abuse, drug addition, petrol sniffing, failed relationships, unplanned pregnancy, shoplifting, relative poverty, sexual assault, and petty crime, only to return to the institution of state prison.

Ultimately, the inter-generational Indigenous inequity culminates to the point where the Aboriginal people end up being in and out of prison, at a climactic point, spending up to 23 hours a day in solitary confinement within an Australian prison cell.[810] Then at the psychological and physical point of no return, when the Aboriginal person is completely broken down; deprived of every aspect of natural liberty, stripped of personal agency, not afforded the legal protection of basic human rights, stripped of individual autonomy, denied access to medical care, constantly remanded in police custody, denied bail for insignificant crimes, and positioned wholly beneath human dignity, then the Aboriginal Australian person only has one destined future—that of death in the British Australian police custody.[811] In the name of the Father, the Son, and the Holy Spirit, Jesus Christ forgive the Anglo-Saxon civilisation for their most evil crimes against the Indigenous Australian people. For such inhumane and cruel crimes are truly beyond the descriptive capacity of words, and most definitely beyond the rational capacity of any member of the human species to unreservedly forgive, Amen.

---

810 As an example, examine the case of Wonyarna Edwards, An Aboriginal man who at 16 was held in solitary confinement in an adult prison for three months and spent up to 23 hours a day in a cell in the state of Victoria.
Wahlquist, Calla. (2018). *Aboriginal man sues over three months' solitary in adult priosn when he was 16*. The Guardian. Date accessed: 22 February 2020. Access link: <https://www.theguardian.com/australia-news/2018/jun/08/aboriginal-man-sues-over-three-months-solitary-in-adult-prison-when-he-was-16>

811 There have been at least 424 confirmed cases of Aboriginal deaths in police custody in Australia since the 1991 Royal Commission into Aboriginal Deaths in Custody. See: Allam, L., Wahlquist, C., and Evershed, N. (2019). *Indigenous deaths in custody worsen in year of tracking by Deaths Inside project*. The Guardian. Date accessed: 22 February 2020. Access link: <https://www.theguardian.com/australia-news/2019/aug/23/Indigenous-deaths-in-custody-worsen-over-year-of-tracking-by-deaths-inside-project>

CHAPTER 6 | HISTORY AND JURISPRUDENCE

The highest truth, the Eternal Truth, in so far as it concerns the black Aboriginal Australian in the white Anglo-Saxon civilisation of the Commonwealth of Australia, is that the predominant place for the Aboriginal people in this foreign and alien British civilisation society is in the institutions of the museum, hospital, state reservation, prison, police custody, or cemetery. Within 232 years, such injustice has been placed upon the Australian Indigenous people and their sacred lands not seen by nature's wrath (i.e., cyclones, droughts, epidemics, famines, tsunamis, pandemics, tornadoes, earthquakes, bushfires, and flash floods) over the past 65,000 years; 'I fmell the bloud of an Englifh-man'.[812] It is a near divine miracle that the Australian Indigenous people continue to exist on the continent of Australia in the twenty-first century. Long endure the just and moral cause of the Aboriginal civilisation on the unlawfully British Crown occupied native Aboriginal land.

It is a regrettable truth that the Aboriginal civilisation of Australia, have been inflicted injustices thrice over; the eighteenth and nineteenth century Anglo-Saxon *genocidal massacre* of the Indigenous Australian people, the twentieth century Anglo-Saxon *involuntary assimilation* of Aboriginal children into Anglo-Saxon families, Christian Church missionaries, and state government reservations, and the twenty-first century Anglo-Saxon *incarceration* of the Indigenous Australian people in the Australian federal, state, and territory prisons. It is an ineradicable truth that the modern British Commonwealth of Australia, stands upon occupied ancient Aboriginal and Torres Strait Islander people's country. Lest we forget.

Notwithstanding the aforementioned discourse on the historical injustices imposed by one racial and ethnic group (i.e., the British civilisation), upon the Indigenous Australians, one cannot reasonably assign blame and infer guilt for past atrocities and injustices unto the present generation of the Anglo-Saxon

---

812 Nashe, Thomas. (1596). *Have with you to Saffron-walden*. London: John Danter, p. 38.

Australian people. For that is to unjustly hold the present generation accountable for the former generation's immoral actions and diabolical crimes against humanity.

However, one can reasonably expect the present [generation of] Anglo-Saxon Australian people to assume moral and legal responsibility for the negative externalities, the outcomes, the inequity of the former generations' government policies, positive laws, and state sanctioned actions. Consequently, the present [generation] must engage in constructive measures, to the best of their ability, to remedy the past injustices against the Indigenous people of Australia.

990

On patriarchy. Historically, the institution of *patriarchy* has been construed as a social system that was traditionally and universally accepted across a multitude of modern nation-states, ancient and contemporary cultures, and distinct ethnic groups, including: Australia, Canada, China, Congo, Egypt, India, Iran, Ireland, Japan, Oman, Saudi Arabia, the United Kingdom of Great Britain and Northern Ireland, and the United States of America. In fact, in the twenty-first century, patriarchy, remains an institutionalised practice of antiquity and continues to function in some parts of the contemporary modern civilised world (i.e., Afghanistan, China, Congo, India, Iran, Iraq, Japan, Nepal, Pakistan, Peru, Saudi Arabia, Sri Lanka, Sudan, Turkey, and Yemen).

However, the Anglo-Saxon and European sovereign nation-states have been subject to the progressive ideological movements of *Secularism*, *Liberalism*, and *Feminism*. With the modern ideology of feminism partially arising as a product of *Democracy* and *Capitalism*, however, contemporary feminism, as an ideology was provisioned substantial global momentum; international support for its cause, that arose out of the two catastrophic twentieth-century world wars, during which women performed an integral part of the domestic production effort within the national war-time economies of the sovereign nation-state (see Figure 52).[813]

In particular, during *World War II* (1939–1945), when significant numbers of working-age and able men were notably absent from the Allied nation-states (i.e., Australia, Great Britain, Canada, France, New Zealand, the United States of America), and served abroad in the navy, military, and air force of the armed forces fighting the belligerent nation-states; the Axis Powers (i.e., the NAZI Germany, Fascist Italy, and Imperial Japan), in order to dutifully engage in the front lines and theatres of war across North Africa, Europe, and the Asia-Pacific, it was the women who performed the historically male-dominated employment roles within the twentieth-century society. A positive externality, that arose out of this catastrophic global conflict, was the provisioning of both the opportunity and capacity for women to more cohesively demonstrate their public integration into overly male-dominated functions of the modern Western civilised society, such as paid full-time employment in factories and shipyards.

During the entire period of the two World Wars, from 1914 to 1945, for the first time in the modern history of the human civilisation, women acted and conducted themselves, in large numbers, independently of the male sex within the public sphere of the modern conventional society. In 1917, Mrs. Raymond Robins, a delegate to the *American Women's Trade Union League Congress* (1917) described it to be 'The first hour in history for the women of the world. This is the woman's age.'[814]

In fact, during the *Great War* (1914–1918) women demonstrated unprecedented functional agency and social autonomy equivalent to that of their male counterparts in the conventional modern Western society. This constituted a watershed moment in respect to the female sex's emancipation movement and global

---

813 *World War I* (1914–1918), and *World War II* (1939–1945).
814 Lemons, J. S. (1973). *The Women Citizen: Social Feminism in the 1920s*. New Haven: Yale University Press, p. 20.

A PHILOSOPHICAL TREATISE OF REALITY | VOLUME III

Figure 52: Rosie the Riveter.
Image Credit: Office for Emergency Management, War Production Board / U.S. National Archives and Records Administration [NARA Identifier: 535413] [Local Identifier: 179-WP-1563].

advocacy for women's rights. For the first time in the human history, the role and responsibilities of the female sex had transitioned from the private sphere into the public domain. This newfound reality for women contributed to the universal female suffrage movement, and resulted in the right to vote for women across the Western, liberal, secular, and democratic modern nation-states.

In addition, what followed was a fundamental economic, political, and social recalibration of the modern Western society. These included the opportunities for women to receive an equal education, the equal right to private property ownership, entrance into the established professions of law, politics, and medicine, and the female's equal legal right to a divorce from her male spouse. The Chinese Communist Party's Chairman Mao Zedong's popular political slogan, that 'Women hold up half the sky' seemed to be gaining serious and credible momentum in the twentieth century Western civilisation.[815]

The female's unequal struggle to be accepted as an equal amongst her male counterparts in the modern conventional society has been a moral and legal endeavour in accordance with the ideation of eternal law. An unequal struggle that has been in progress for over four centuries, and remains an objective to be wholly realised in the twenty-first century.[816, 817] However, within the contemporary modern civilised world, the accomplishments and socio-economic progress that the female sex has made, and continues to make, in the predominantly white Anglo-Saxon, Christian, and 'man-

---

815   Zedong, Mao. (J. K. Leung, and M. Y. M. Kau, Eds.) (1992). *The Writings of Mao Zedong 1949–1976. Volume II: January 1956- December 1957.* New York: M. E. Sharpe, p. 558.
816   In 1718, Sweden became the first country to permit tax-paying female members of city guilds to be permitted to vote in local city elections and national elections.
817   In the twenty-first century, in the Kingdom of Saudi Arabia, women are restricted in their capacity to act as independent and autonomous citizens due to the nation's male guardianship system. See: Human Rights Watch. (2019). *Saudi Arabia: 10 Reasons Why Women Flee.* Human Rights Watch. Date accessed: 29 July 2019. Access link: <https://www.hrw.org/news/2019/01/30/saudi-arabia-10-reasons-why-women-flee>

made' economic, political, legal, medical, and social institutional structures, at both the international and national level, of the conventional modern society is promising, for a more equitable future between the sexes in the human society:

- In 1553, *Mary I* (r. 1553–1558) became England's first female monarch.
- In 1558, *Elizabeth I* (r. 1558–1603) was appointed to the English monarchy, and is considered to be one of the greatest monarchs of England.
- In 1678, *Elena Cornaro Piscopia* became the first female to complete a Ph.D. (University Doctoral Degree) at the University of Padua, Italy.
- In 1762, *Catherine II* (Catherine the Great) was crowned empress regnant of All Russia, a sovereign position of supreme power that she held until 1796.
- In 1811, *Jane Austen* completed and published her first novel *Sense and Sensibility*. This literary achievement was followed by Austen's subsequent novel *Pride and Prejudice* which was published in 1813.
- In 1828, *Sojourner Truth*, a former slave, became the first African American woman to win a legal case for the custody of her son in a U.S. court of law against an American man. Truth was a passionate African American abolitionist and women's rights advocate; she is well known for her 'Ain't I A Woman?' speech delivered at the Ohio Women's Rights Convention in 1851.
- In 1835, *Mary Somerville* and *Caroline Herschel* became the first two women to be jointly admitted as members of the Royal Astronomical Society.
- In 1840, *Lucretia Mott* attended the World's Anti-Slavery Convention in London. Among Mott's numerous achievements in the women's rights movement and the abolition of slavery campaign, she organised the Seneca Falls Convention in New

CHAPTER 6 | HISTORY AND JURISPRUDENCE

York in 1848. In addition, Mott also founded the Philadelphia Female Anti-Slavery Society in 1833.

- In 1843, *Ada Lovelace* published an academic paper in an English science journal that made significant contributions to the field of modern computing science.
- In 1848, *Elizabeth Cady Stanton* authored the Declaration of Sentiments at the Seneca Falls Convention in New York. In Stanton's voluminous writings and lifelong work, she advocated for the equality of all men and women.
- In 1849, *Elizabeth Blackwell* became the first female to earn a Medical Degree at the Geneva Medical College, New York City.
- In 1860, *Florence Nightingale* established Saint Thomas' Hospital and the Nightingale Training School for Nurses. Nightingale, also known as 'the Lady with the Lamp' is the founder of modern nursing.
- In 1869, *Susan B. Anthony* founded the National Woman Suffrage Association. Anthony made significant contributions to the women's rights movement in the United States of America, in particular the right of women to vote, she also campaigned for the abolition of slavery.
- In 1901, *Annie Jump Cannon* published a simplified classification scheme of 1,122 stars, Cannon's spectral classifications have been universally adopted in the field of Astronomy. In addition, Cannon also discovered ca. 300 variable Stars and 5 Novae. For her contribution to Astronomy, Cannon was the first woman to be awarded an Honorary Doctorate from the University of Oxford in 1925.
- In 1908, *Henrietta Swan Leavitt* discovered a relationship between the period and the luminosity in a certain class of visible stars.
- In 1918, *Emmy Noether* discovered that if the Lagrangian does not change in time, when the coordinate system changes, then there is a quantity of energy that is reserved. Her finding

became known as the Noether Theorem, a key component of Theoretical Physics.
- In 1925, *Cecilia Payne-Gaposchkin* discovered that stars are predominantly composed of two of the lightest chemical elements—Hydrogen and Helium.
- In 1931, *Jane Addams* won the Nobel Peace Prize for her dedication to the peace movement and social work. Addams was the first American women to receive the aforesaid prestigious honour.
- In 1933, *Sophonisba Preston Breckinridge* became the first woman to represent the U.S. government in an international diplomatic conference, when she was sent as a delegate to the 7th Pan-American Conference in Uruguay.
- In 1935, *Irène Joliot-Curie* was awarded the Nobel Prize in Chemistry for her joint discovery (with her husband, Jean Frédéric Joliot-Curie) of artificial radioactivity.
- In 1939, *Lise Meitner* in connexion with Otto Frisch wrote to the Editor of the premier international scientific journal—*Nature*—describing the phenomenon of Nuclear Fission in Physics. In addition, Meitner, in connexion with Otto Hanh, jointly made the discovery of Barium, however, Hanh alone received the prestigious international recognition for this novel (and joint) discovery, and thus, Hanh was the awarded the 1944 Nobel Prize in Chemistry.
- In 1941, *Helen Brooke Taussig* proposed a novel medical operation to assist new born infants with the medical condition of 'Blue Baby Syndrome'. On 9 November 1944, Helen Taussig and her colleagues performed an operation on a child with Anoxemia, the operation was successful, and it was thereafter repeated on two other infants with the same medical condition, the technique was named 'The Blalock-Taussig Operation'.[818]

---

818 U.S. National Library of Medicine. (2003). *Biography: Dr. Helen Brooke Taussig*. U.S. National Library of Medicine. Date accessed: 25 November 2020. Access link: <https://cfmedicine.nlm.nih.gov/physicians/biography_316.html >

Taussig's entire accomplishments are too numerous to acknowledge herein, however, she was a founder of the medical subspeciality known as 'Pediatric Cardiology', she was a recipient of the U.S. Medal of Freedom in 1964 from the U.S. President Lyndon B. Johnson, and was also elected as the President of the American Heart Association in 1965.

- In 1942, *Hedwig Kiesler*, in connexion with George Antheil, was awarded a U.S. Patent for the creation of a new communication system that could engage in transmitter and receiver hopping of radio waves.
- In 1951, *Esther Miriam Zimmer Lederberg* published her discovery of Lambda phage; a virus that infects E. coli bacteria. Lederberg's applied research also created the foundation for the demonstration of how phages transfer genes between bacteria. In spite of Lederberg's exemplary contributions to the field of medicine, and her co-contribution to applied scientific research, her first husband, Joshua Lederberg received the 1958 Nobel Prize in Physiology or Medicine.
- In 1952, *Rosalind Elsie Franklin* (see Figure 53), in connexion with Raymond Gosling, captured an X-ray diffraction image of paracrystalline gel composed of DNA fiber known as Photo 51. Unbeknown to Franklin, her scientific research was utilised by James Watson and Francis Crick, in connection with their own data to create their famous DNA model (see Figure 54), and the two male biologists published their findings in a key academic paper in 1953.

  Franklin's original contribution to the discovery of DNA's structure was not acknowledged, nor was she jointly awarded 'The Nobel Prize in Physiology or Medicine' in 1962 for this scientific milestone in the human understanding of the DNA Double Helix structure which was awarded to Crick, Watson, and Wilkins.
- In 1955, Rosa Parks refused to give up her passenger seat to an American man on a segregated bus in Montgomery, Alabama.

Figure 53: The British scientist Rosalind Elsie Franklin.
Image Credit: World History Archive / Alamy.

CHAPTER 6 | HISTORY AND JURISPRUDENCE

Figure 54: Watson and Crick discover the structure of DNA.
Image Credit: Science Photo Library / Alamy.

Parks' courage and bravery led to the Montgomery Bus Boycott which lasted a total of 381 days. Not to mention, the greater social, political, economic, and legal change that resulted from this boycott movement for the African American people. The Montgomery Bus Boycott ultimately ended with a U.S. Supreme Court ruling that declared segregation on U.S. public transport to be unconstitutional.

- In 1960, *Sirimavo Bandaranaike* of Sri Lanka became the first female elected Prime Minister of a modern nation-state.
- In 1961, *Katherine Johnson* was the first women, not to mention, an African-American women, to calculate the trajectory for the 5 May 1961 space flight of Alan Shepard, the first American sent into outer space. In addition, Johnson calculated the launch window for Shephard's 1961 Mercury mission.
- In 1964, *Dorothy Crowfoot Hodgkin* was awarded the Nobel Prize for Chemistry for her determination of the complicated structure of Vitamin B12. Hodgkin also made original contributions to human scientific knowledge concerning the crystallography of biochemical compounds.
- In 1973, *Billie Jean King* defeated Bobby Riggs in the 'Battle of the Sexes', 6-4, 6-3, 6-3. King has 39 Grand Slam titles to her name; this includes a record 20 titles at Wimbledon.
- In 1981, *Sandra Day O'Connor* became the first female in the history of the United States of America to be appointed as an Associate Justice to the U.S. Supreme Court.
- In 1997, *Madeleine Jana Korbel Albright* became the first female U.S. Secretary of State.
- In 2005, *Angela Merkel* became the first female Chancellor of Germany.
- In 2008, *Ann E. Dunwoody* became the first woman in the U.S. military history to achieve a four-star General rank.
- In 2014, *Janet Louise Yellen* became the first female Chair of the U.S. Federal Reserve Bank.

- In 2016, *Mother Mary Teresa* was canonised as Saint Teresa of Calcutta by the Roman Catholic Church.
- In 2017, *Susan Mary Kiefel* became the first female justice to be appointed to the position of the Honourable Chief Justice of the High Court of Australia.
- In 2019, Major General *Alenka Ermenc* became the first female Chief of the Armed Forces of a modern sovereign nation-state (the Republic of Slovenia).
- In 2019, *Christine Lagarde* became the first female President of the European Central Bank, not to mention, she was the first women to become France's Finance Minister (2007–2011), and also the first women managing director of the International Monetary Fund (2011–2019).

The modern feminist movement has now shifted towards the final two frontiers, which remain subject to exclusive male jurisdiction in the contemporary modern civilised society; the *status quo* 'political' and 'religious' institutions. In respect to the former, women are increasingly seeking and being elected to the highest positions of public office and civil government within their sovereign nation-states.[819] In relation to the latter, women are now overturning established religious precedents, doctrines, ideologies, theological practices, and time-honoured normative precepts of the Church, by seeking priestly ordination into the Church; a traditionally exclusive male-dominated role within the clergy.[820]

Notwithstanding, in the late twentieth-century, women have been successful in making substantial progress and history in this respect. Herein, the Church of England is a classic case study in

---

819 In the twenty-first century; Prime Minister of Australia Julia Gillard (2010), Chancellor of Germany Angela Merkel (2005), Prime Minister of the United Kingdom Theresa May (2016), and Prime Minister of New Zealand Jacinda Ardern (2017).

820 'Once made equal to man, woman becomes his superior.' Socrates (ca. 470 BCE – ca. 399 BCE). See: Rogers, James Tullis. (1968). *The Codicil. The University of Michigan Law School. Class Year Publications*, Paper 182, p. 4.

point. In 1994 the aforesaid Church ordained its first-ever female priests, with thirty-two female priests.[821] This act overturned half a millennium of religious tradition within the Church of England that promoted men to select positions within the Church on the exclusive basis of sex.

In addition, in 2014, the Church of England formally approved legislation permitting the appointment of female bishops, a move that is in direct contradiction with Christian doctrine.[822] Not to mention, that such legislation was incompatible with the official directive of the Roman Catholic Church, as stipulated by Pope John Paul II (1920–2005) in his 1994 Apostolic Letter, that banned the ordination of women into the Roman Catholic Church.[823]

In the final analysis, the two remaining noble positions to be targeted by women within the Church of England and the Roman Catholic Church are the Archbishop of Canterbury and the Pope, respectively. In all likelihood, if the former 330 years of the modern history is any enlightening guide, women will conquer these two remaining positions, reminiscent of gender-based inequality, by the end of the twenty-second century! Ultimately, the once traditional, conservative, orthodox, institutionalised, and universal concept of the *Sexus Sequior* (the second sex) will become ever more marginalised within the postmodern conventional human society.

---

821   Darnton, John. (1994). *After 460 Years, The Anglicans Ordain Women*. The New York Times. Date accessed: 31 March 2019. Access link: <https://www.nytimes.com/1994/03/13/world/after-460-years-the-anglicans-ordain-women.html>

822   Williams, Alex. (2019). *25 years of women priests in the Church of England celebrated*. Premier. Date accessed: 31 March 2019. Access link: <https://www.premier.org.uk/News/UK/25-years-of-women-priests-in-the-Church-of-England-celebrated>

823   Pope John Paul II. (1994). *Apostolic Letter Ordinatio Sacerdotalis*. Libreria Editrice Vaticana. Libreria Editrice Vaticana. Date accessed: 31 March 2019. Access link: <https://w2.vatican.va/content/john-paul-ii/en/apost_letters/1994/documents/hf_jp-ii_apl_19940522_ordinatio-sacerdotalis.html>

991

On the institution of law. Positive law is an instrument of the elite, powerful, influential, lettered, and opulent aristocratic class of the conventional human society. The 'force of law' is one of the means and instruments by which the aristocratic class create the 'legal authority' to ensure the poor working-class masses remain obedient and subservient to the aristocracy's economic interests in the conventional society.[824]

In addition, the operative principles of common law and constitutional law in a sovereign nation-state, can be suspended from ordinary operation at any point in time, in order to lawfully employ lethal force against the poor working-class masses to quash disobedience, to demand that the poor, ignorant, and unlettered masses obey what is most desirable and of economic self-interest to the rich and powerful aristocratic class, by recourse to the legal mechanisms of martial law, state of emergency powers, military rule, and rule by presidential or royal decree.

The institution of law functions and serves those constituents on whose side it stands, and it serves to legitimise and sanction the use of force for that particular party. Needless to infer, the antagonist, the seditionist, the secessionist, is portrayed as a symbol of aggression and can be inferred to be a 'terrorist' within the sovereign and independent nation-state. Thus, the incumbent sovereign engages in anti-terrorism and counter-terrorism operations to prevent a 'breach of the peace' and uphold the sovereign nation-state's 'national security' interests, to eliminate unwanted threats to its supreme position of sovereign power under the pretext of an eternal duty, an oath, to 'keep the peace' and restore 'law and order' in the sovereign

---

824 Cardinal Armand Jean du Plessis, Duke of Richelieu. (1585–1642). 'Harshness towards individuals who flout the laws and commands of the state is for the public good; no greater crime against the public interest is possible than to show leniency to those who violate it.' See: Knecht, R. J. (1991). *Richelieu*. New York: Routledge Publication, p. 129.

nation-state. Regardless, be it an unjust peace and oppressive order in the conventional reality. Political methods that can be employed to achieve such desirable ends of the incumbent sovereign and the political constituents include: solitary confinement, incarceration, corporal punishment, capital punishment, substantial monetary fines, imprisonment terms, good behaviour bonds, or community service.[825]

992

On the enduring injustices inflicted and served upon the Indigenous Aboriginal people, the Torres Strait Islander people, the Māori people, and the American Indian people of the 'settled British Commonwealth countries', by the Anglo-Saxon and the European civilisations.[826] The first component of this philosophical thesis analyses the modern history of the matter and the contemporary problem. The second component proposes a practical resolution to the intractable historical legacy of the British and European settlement and colonisation of sacred Indigenous lands.

First, the native Indigenous civilisations across the Commonwealth of Australia, the Dominion of Canada, New Zealand, and the United States of America, were severely depopulated by their involuntary contact with the Anglo-Saxon and European people, and the negative externality associated with the introduction of Western diseases (i.e., Smallpox, Measles, and Influenza), and the modern Western lifestyle. Not in any manner to lessen the associated impact of the intentional genocidal British and European

---

825 'Whether the government acts with moderation or with cruelty, there are always different degrees of punishment; major or minor penalties are applied to major or minor crimes. The imagination adjusts itself automatically to the customs of the country that one is in.' See: Montesquieu. (C. J. Betts, Trans.) (1973). *Persian Letters*. London: Pengiun Classics, p. 159.
826 the Commonwealth of Australia, the Dominion of Canada, New Zealand, and the United States of America.

CHAPTER 6 | HISTORY AND JURISPRUDENCE

practices employed against the Indigenous population on the foreign Indigenous lands.

Second, the surviving Indigenous population was forcefully assimilated into the Anglo-Saxon civilisation; subject to zoned state government reservations, enslaved to toil, institutionalised into Christian missionaries, lawfully had their biological children forcibly removed and integrated into the Anglo-Saxon families.[827] All such methods executed in a systematic attempt to eradicate the 'way of life' of the Indigenous people, and the future human regenerative capacity of the native population's distinct gene pool. The Indigenous populations hunter-gatherer society, their lifestyle, language, history, traditions, customs, beliefs, practices, laws, historical artefacts, and culture were fundamentally decimated; what collectively has conclusively been determined to constitute a 'breach of fundamental human rights' of the Indigenous people in the Commonwealth of Australia.[828]

In effect, the grand immoral aim of the British civilisation was to render the Aboriginal civilisation extinct, period. As the British civilisation was ultimately unsuccessful in their genocidal endeavour, what they have incidentally created, is the negative externality of the 'Aboriginal problem' in the Commonwealth of Australia, the 'Māori problem' in New Zealand, and the 'American Indian problem' in the Dominion of Canada and the United States of America.

Third, in the particular case of the Commonwealth of Australia, the application of Aboriginal Indigenous customary laws

---

[827] Between 1910–1970, many Indigenous children were forcibly removed from their families as a result of various government policies. The generations of children removed under these policies became known as the Stolen Generations. See: Australians Together. (2019). *The Stolen Generations*. Australians Together. Date accessed: 11 April 2019. Access link: <https://australianstogether.org.au/discover/australian-history/stolen-generations>

[828] Commonwealth of Australia. (1997). *Bringing them home: National Inquiry into the Separation of Aboriginal and Torres Strait Islander Children from their families*. Commonwealth of Australia. Date accessed: 11 April 2019. Access link: <https://www.humanrights.gov.au/sites/default/files/content/pdf/social_justice/bringing_them_home_report.pdf>

and sacred traditions on their own native territory was suspended, void, and declared inoperable since the inception of the British Crown's fictitious legal doctrine of *Terra Nullius* (Nobody's Land) in 1788. In their place, the implementation of foreign English common law derived from the British Crown and the sovereign British Parliament, received precedence and legal recognition in Australia.[829] That is to infer, the British legislation was deemed operable by the extraterritorial acts of the United Kingdom's Imperial Parliament which possessed the 'force of law' in the overseas British Commonwealth territories.[830]

Fourth, the Aboriginal people of Australia were lynched, incarcerated, hanged, shot, enslaved, raped, massacred, and tortured during the eighteenth and nineteenth centuries. Such barbaric, uncivilised, and inhumane actions by the British civilisation against the Indigenous civilisation, amounts to crimes against humanity; mass atrocity crimes that are genocidal in nature.[831] Such immoral actions were undertaken by the Anglo-Saxon civilisation's concentrated effort to further the whole extermination of the original inhabitants; the native Indigenous people of the Commonwealth of Australia.

In addition, the Aboriginal people have been subject to numerous deaths in Australian police custody, including in the twentieth century and into the twenty-first century.[832] As examples,

---

[829] In 1829, British sovereignty extended to cover the whole of Australia—every person born in Australia, including Aboriginal and Torres Strait Islander people, became a British subject by birth.

[830] On 25 July 1828, the *Australian Courts Act 1828* came into force. It enacted legislation of the British Parliament which ensured that the laws of England would be applied in the two existing Australian colonies, New South Wales and Van Diemen's Land.

[831] Ryan, Lyndall. (2008). Massacre in the Black War in Tasmania 1823–1834: a case study of the Meander River Region, June 1827. *Journal of Genocide Research*. Volume 10, No. 4, pp. 479–499.

[832] In 2004, Mr. Mulrunji Doomadgee died in custody on Palm Island, Queensland after being arrested for public drunkenness. In 2008, Mr. Ian Ward died in custody in Western Australia after being arrested for a traffic offence. In 2014, Ms. Julieka Ivanna Dhu died in custody in Western Australia after being arrested

consider the death of the Aboriginal Australian, Lloyd James Boney who was violently arrested on 6 August 1987 by Australian police officers for the breach of his bail conditions, Boney was found dead in police custody 90 minutes later, hanging by a football sock in an Australian police cell.[833] Furthermore, consider the case of the Aboriginal Australian, David Dungay Junior, a 26-year-old Indigenous male, who died at Sydney's Long Bay Prison in December 2015.

In fact, such hideous and culpable conduct is tacitly sanctioned, endorsed, and made permissible, given no criminal conviction, punishment, or prison sentence, has ever been recorded, or provisioned against a police officer of Anglo-Saxon descent or European ancestry, for the unjust and preventable death of an unarmed black Aboriginal Australian person in police custody in the Commonwealth of Australia in the twentieth century.[834]

In the twenty-first century, the Aboriginal Australian people continue to experience, cruel, inhumane, and degrading treatment by the predominantly white Anglo-Saxon race comprised Australian Federal, State, and Territory Police Forces. The Aboriginal Australian experiences the depravity of freedom both in life and death in the Anglo-Saxon (foreign and alien British) modern conventional

---

for unpaid fines. In sum, the aforementioned cases are not isolated, more than 400 Aboriginal and Torres Strait Islander people have died in custody since the end of the Royal Commission into Aboriginal Deaths in Custody (RCIADIC) in 1991. See: The Guardian. (2018). *Deaths inside: Indigenous Australian deaths in custody*. The Guardian. Date accessed: 7 July 2019. Access link: <https://www.theguardian.com/australia-news/ng-interactive/2018/aug/28/deaths-inside-Indigenous-australian-deaths-in-custody>

833   Anthony, Thalia. (2016). *Deaths in custody: 25 years after the royal commission, we've gone backwards*. The Conversation. Date accessed: 22 October 2020. Access link: <https://theconversation.com/deaths-in-custody-25-years-after-the-royal-commission-weve-gone-backwards-57109>

834   AustLII Indigenous Law Resources. (1998). *Royal Commission into Aboriginal Deaths in Custody*. Reconciliation and Social Justice Library. Date accessed: 11 April 2019. Access link: <http://www.austlii.edu.au/au/other/IndigLRes/rciadic/>

society supplanted upon the native Aboriginal land in the Commonwealth of Australia.[835]

One's human conscience, morality, and intellect ought to be at pains to ascertain why an unconscious, unarmed, and uneducated Aboriginal Australian person is treated beneath the universal value of human dignity? Decency which ought to be blindly afforded to all constituents of the British Commonwealth of Australia is absent for the Aboriginal Australian people. Sam Watson Senior, an Aboriginal rights campaigner has asserted that, 'Not a single police officer in any criminal jurisdiction in the Commonwealth has ever been convicted of any offence relating to an Aboriginal death in custody'.[836] Does this reality appear to constitute legal immunity for the white Anglo-Saxon descent *second* Australians to kill the *first* black Indigenous Australians? Is this unequal treatment of Indigenous Australians simply a matter of racial prejudice? How many Royal Commissions of Inquiry are needed in the Commonwealth of Australia to create a fundamental shift in the attitudes of the second Anglo-Saxon Australians towards the traditional custodians of Ngunnawal Country and Arnhem Land?

Lest we forget, if the Aboriginal Australian person dares to assert the inalienable sovereign rights vested in the First Nations Peoples of Australia, that is to infer, attempts to resist against the deprivation of one's fundamental political right to self-determination and human freedom, then the Aboriginal Australian will be oppressed by the Anglo-Saxon Australian with the use of lethal force; apprehended and tasered to one's knees, taken into the Anglo-Australian police custody, sent to the institution of the state prison, or the medical hospital, or even murdered in cold-blood in the policy custody by

---

835 Hawke, Sarah. (2017). *Family calls for investigation after Eric Whittaker died shackled by his ankles in a Sydney hospital bed*. ABC News. Date accessed: 12 August 2019. Access link: <https://www.abc.net.au/news/2017-12-03/eric-whittakers-family-calls-for-review-of-death-in-custody/9221266>

836 Korff, Jens. (2019). *Aboriginal-police relations*. Creative Spirits. Date accessed: 30 November 2019. Access link: <https://www.creativespirits.info/aboriginalculture/law/aboriginal-police-relations>

those Anglo-Saxon police officers of the British Commonwealth whose sworn duty it is to presumably to 'serve and protect' the Australian people.[837]

In addition, the reader is strongly urged to investigate the *2007 Northern Territory Intervention* ('NT Intervention') under the leadership of the Prime Minister of Australia, the Right Honourable John Winston Howard (r. 1996–2007). The NT Intervention was a set of paternalistic policies instituted by the Commonwealth Government in Australia pursuant to the *Northern Territory National Emergency Response Act 2007 (Cth)* to deprive the Aboriginal Australian people of their freedom, dignity, self-determination, human rights, native land, natural resources, and biological children. The Howard Government's moral basis for the NT Intervention was *The Little Children are Sacred Report 2007*. However, the NT Intervention only addressed 2 out of the 97 recommendations stipulated in this Northern Territory Government report.[838]

In 2010, the NT Intervention was investigated by the United Nations (UN). The UN appointed independent expert, Special Rapporteur James Anaya, compiled his findings in the *'Report by the Special Rapporteur on the situation of human rights and fundamental freedoms of Indigenous people'*.[839] The UN report concluded that 'several aspects of the NT Intervention racially discriminated against Indigenous Australians and violated their basic human rights.'[840]

---

837 The Guardian. (2017). *Clifton Penny filmed shaking in hospital nine days after being tasered—video*. The Guardian. Date accessed: 12 August 2019. Access link: <https://www.theguardian.com/global/video/2017/jan/20/clifton-penny-filmed-shaking-in-hospital-nine-days-after-being-tasered-video>

838 Australians Together. (2020). *The Intervention: A controversial policy package*. Australians Together. Date accessed: 19 December 2020. Access link: <https://australianstogether.org.au/discover/the-wound/the-intervention/>

839 United Nations Human Rights Council. (2010). *Report by the Speical Rapporteur on the situation of human rights and fundamental freedoms of Indigenous people*. A/ HRC/ 15/ 37/ Add.4. United Nations Human Rights Council. Date accessed: 19 December 2020. Access link: <http://unsr.jamesanaya.org/docs/special/2010_special_australia_en.pdf>

840 Australians Together. (2020). *The Intervention: A controversial policy package*. Australians Together. Date accessed: 19 December 2020.

Now, in order to ensure the black Aboriginal Australian people will not have the right of equality before the Australian law, that is to infer, the Aboriginal people shall be denied recourse to the relief of the Australian common law, the white Anglo-Saxon people successfully amended the Commonwealth law, in order to legally permit racial discrimination against the black Aboriginal Australian people. Why? Well, firstly, this immoral and racist practice should be of no surprise to the reader. If it is, then the reader ought to inquire into *The White Australia Policy (1901–1973)*. And this is how the white Anglo-Australian people did it … The suspension of the operating provisions prescribed within the *Racial Discrimination Act 1975 (Cth)*.

As previously noted, the Howard Government passed the Northern Territory National Emergency Response (NTER) legislation, namely:

- *Northern Territory National Emergency Response Act 2007 (Cth)*
- *Social Security and Other Legislation Amendment (Welfare Payment Reform) Act 2007 (Cth)*
- *Families, Community Services and Indigenous Affairs and Other Legislation Amendment (Northern Territory National Emergency Response and Other Measures) Act 2007 (Cth)*
- *Appropriation (Northern Territory National Emergency Response) Act (No. 1) 2007–2008 2007 (Cth)*
- *Appropriation (Northern Territory National Emergency Response) Act (No. 2) 2007–2008 2007 (Cth)*

The concern with the passage of the aforementioned legislation was that it breached the letter and spirit of the *Racial Discrimination Act 1975 (Cth)* (the 'RD Act'). For Part II of the RD Act forbids racial discrimination, as stipulated in the subsections 9(1), and 9(1A) of the RD Act. Furthermore, the right to equality before the law is

---

Access link: <https://australianstogether.org.au/discover/the-wound/the-intervention/>

enshrined in Section 10 of the RD Act. Now in order the circumvent the operating provisions of the RD Act, the white Anglo-Saxon people suspended the operation of Part II of the RD Act. Thus, explicitly denying the black Aboriginal Australian people the legal protection provided by the RD Act, and thereby, preventing the possibility of a successful legal challenge to the NTER legislation in the Australian law courts (i.e., the independent function of the Australian judiciary was rendered an ineffective instrument).[841]

Regardless of what the intentions of the NTER legislation were, the facts and outcomes of the legislation point to a complete failure to protect, improve, or further the lives of the Aboriginal Australian people. For example, consider that since the 2007 NT Intervention, domestic violence has increased in Aboriginal communities in the Northern Territory, and the incarceration of the Aboriginal Australian people under 18 years of age is at its highest levels. Not to mention, that according to the former Australian Human Rights Commissioner Professor Gillian Doreen Triggs, 'there has been a 500 per cent increase in Indigenous youth suicide since the years 2007-2011'.[842] Professor of Law Gillian Triggs also acknowledges that the NT Intervention measures breach not only *the Racial Discriminiation Act 1975 (Cth)*, but that it also violates international law; *the United Nations Convention on the Rights of the Child 1989*, and *the United Nations Declaration on the Rights of Indigenous Peoples 2007*.[843]

---

841   Australian Human Rights Commission. (2020). *The Suspension and Reinstatement of the RDA and Special Measures in the NTER*. Australian Human Rights Commission. Date accessed: 19 December 2020. Access link: <https://humanrights.gov.au/our-work/suspension-and-reinstatement-rda-and-special-measures-nter-0#_edn8>

842   Zhou, Naaman. (2017). *Northern Territory intervention violates international law, Gillian Triggs says*. The Guardian. Date accessed: 19 December 2020. Access link: <https://www.theguardian.com/australia-news/2017/sep/02/northern-territory-intervention-violates-international-law-gillian-triggs-says>

843   Zhou, Naaman. (2017). *Northern Territory intervention violates international law, Gillian Triggs says*. The Guardian. Date accessed: 19 December 2020. Access link: <https://www.theguardian.com/australia-news/2017/sep/02/northern-

Notwithstanding the injustices and inequalities that have been institutionalised upon the black Aboriginal Australian people and their communities in the Northern Territory, arising from the introduction of the NTER legislation, and the NT Intervention, the racial oppression continues. In 2012, the Gillard Government successfully passed *the Stronger Futures in the Northern Territory Act 2012*. This legislation was a political measure that was designed to extend the Commonwealth's Northern Territory Intervention mandate that was established by the Howard Government's NTER legislation (which was due to expire in 2012), for a further 10 years, until the year 2022. The three principal acts of *the Stronger Futures in the Northern Territory Act 2012* include:

- *Stronger Futures in the Northern Territory Act 2012*
- *Stronger Futures in the Northern Territory (Consequential and Transitional Provisions) Act 2012*
- *Social Security Legislation Amendment Act 2012*

Furthermore on the topic of the racial oppression of the black Aboriginal Australian people, now understand that the death penalty no longer operates in the legal jurisdiction of the Commonwealth of Australia; its states or territories.[844] However, the death penalty allegedly appears to apply to the Aboriginal person in the contemporary modern Australian society, with complete immunity to the sworn Anglo-Saxon Australian police officer of the British Crown who upholds and enforces the British Commonwealth law on occupied Aboriginal land.[845] That is, the real administration of

---

territory-intervention-violates-international-law-gillian-triggs-says>

844   On 11 March 2010, with bipartisan support, the Commonwealth Parliament of Australia passed the *Crimes Legislation Amendment (Torture Prohibition and Death Penalty Abolition) Act*. This Act amends the *Death Penalty Abolition Act 1973* (Cth) to extend the current Commonwealth prohibition on the death penalty to all States and Territories. This forecloses the possibility of any individual Australian State or Territory jurisdiction reintroducing the death penalty.

845   407 Indigenous Australians have died since the end of the Royal Commission into deaths in custody in 1991. See: Allam, Lorena., Wahlquist, Calla., and

CHAPTER 6 | HISTORY AND JURISPRUDENCE

the unlawful death penalty unto the Aboriginal person is permitted, without the function, rather, the absolute transgression, of 'due process' and the 'rule of law' in the British Commonwealth of Australia.[846]

Pause and peruse the aforementioned words very carefully, what this aforesaid assertion is referring to is the unlawful and unconstitutional killing of the black Aboriginal Australian people. To be precise, the killing of 440 Aboriginal people in Australian police protective custody in the British Commonwealth of Australia, since the 1991 *Royal Commission into Aboriginal Deaths in Custody*.[847] As contemporary examples of the Aboriginal people's deaths in police custody in the British Commonwealth of Australia, consider the following cases:

- The 2017 case of Yorta Yorta Aboriginal woman, Tanya Day, aged 55, who was found dead in a Castlemaine police cell after sustaining a brain injury. Ms. Day had been arrested by the police for public drunkenness.
- The 2020 case of Yorta Yorta Aboriginal woman, Veronica Maine Nelson Walker, aged 37, who was found dead in a maximum-security jail cell at the Dame Phyllis Frost Centre. Ms. Walker was refused bail and remanded in custody; her alleged crime was shoplifting.

Evershed, Nick. (2018). *The 147 dead: terrible toll of Indigenous deaths in custody spurs call for reform*. The Guardian. Date accessed: 17 August 2019. Access link: <https://www.theguardian.com/australia-news/2018/aug/28/the-147-dead-Indigenous-leaders-demand-action-over-unacceptable-deaths-in-custody>

846   In March 1987, the now-defunct Committee to Defend Black Rights began counting Aboriginal deaths in custody as part of a national campaign. It found one Indigenous person died while incarcerated every 11 days. See: Anthony, Thalia. (2016). *Deaths in custody: 25 years after the royal commission, we've gone backwards*. The Conversation. Date accessed: 17 August 2019. Access link: <https://theconversation.com/deaths-in-custody-25-years-after-the-royal-commission-weve-gone-backwards-57109>

847   Young, Evan. (2021). *After three new Indigenous deaths in custody, justice campaigners ask: 'where is the outrage?'*. SBS News Australia. Date accessed: 13 March 2021. Access link: <https://www.sbs.com.au/news/after-three-new-indigenous-deaths-in-custody-justice-campaigners-ask-where-is-the-outrage>

By no means are the two aforementioned cases isolated examples. The unlawful killing of the black Aboriginal Australian people, to be precise, of 440 black Aboriginal Australian people, from 1991 to 2021, is a common occurrence, that is to infer, it is a racist, prejudiced, biased, discriminatory, and systematic part of the criminal justice system in the British Commonwealth of Australia, what was once White Australia (1901–1973).[848] Ask yourself the fundamental question concerning the deliverance of natural justice at English common law. Would a white Christian Anglo-Saxon descent second Australian be killed in Australian police custody, let alone denied bail and remanded in prison for petty crimes (i.e., shoplifting, public drunkenness, motor vehicle related offences, good order offences, or public nuisance offences)?

Consequentially, one must seriously inquire into the following vexed question—In the particular case of the Aboriginal person in the British Commonwealth of Australia, does the punishment fit the alleged crime? The fundamental legal principle of proportionality does not appear to equitably apply to the Indigenous Australians, to the same extent and degree as it would be universally afforded to the non-Indigenous Australians, in the unjust enforcement of Australian common law.

For ultimately, in both the aforementioned cases perused in this thesis (namely those of Ms. Day and Ms. Walker), the petty crimes committed by the Aboriginal Australian people resulted in the enforcement of the unlawful and unconstitutional death penalty unjustly levied against the Aboriginal Australian. It is more likely than not, that a non-Indigenous Australian would not have received the same outcome (that of death) from a trivial offence against the

---

[848] For additional examples of Aboriginal deaths in police custody see: Deaths Inside Database. (2019). *Indigenous Australian deaths in custody 2019.* The Guardian. Date accessed: 22 February 2020. Access link: <https://www.theguardian.com/australia-news/ng-interactive/2018/aug/28/deaths-inside-Indigenous-australian-deaths-in-custody>

Anglo-Australian common law. Thus, are all Australian citizens—Indigenous and non-Indigenous—treated with equality before the English common law in the British Commonwealth of Australia?

The dismal fact is that the people of the Aboriginal civilisation have been killed in Australia since the advent of the British civilisation in Australia in the eighteenth century. Fundamentally the two distinct civilisations are considerably divergent in their way of life, culture, society, language, ideology, history, values, customs, beliefs, morals, laws, identity, traditions, and heritage. This is the fundamental challenge that needs to be transcended in order to achieve real reconciliation between the ancient Aboriginal civilisation and the modern British civilisation. The challenge of creating respect and equality between two most distinct civilisations on one continent is practically monumental, although not strictly nigh impossible.

To return to the more immediate theme of injustice against the Aboriginal person, the escalation of conflict between the Indigenous Aboriginal and the Anglo-Saxon British Crown Police Officer, the latter who attempts to keep and preserve Her Majesty's Peace in the British Commonwealth of Australia, is divided and polarised upon the grounds of racial segregation in the British Commonwealth of Australia. In a confrontation between the two opposing parties, shall there exist no other lawful or legitimate purpose for the use of force by the Anglo-Saxon Australian police officers involved in their confrontation with an Aboriginal Australian person, then subsequently, the British Crown police officer will arrest and place trumped-up charges against the Aboriginal Australian; with the criminal offences of 'resisting arrest', or 'failing to obey police directions', or 'assaulting a police officer', with the full force of the British Commonwealth of Australia's laws, which are themselves a functional legal derivative of the Sovereign British Crown's Imperial Parliament.[849, 850, 851]

Thus, the Anglo-Saxon Commonwealth system appears to provide complete immunity to the white Christian Anglo-Saxon man, a sort of *carte blanche*, to beat the black Aboriginal man to his bloody death in the Australian police custody.[852] In the event that the Anglo-Saxon police officer determines not to discharge or employ lethal and deadly force to immediately kill the Aboriginal Australian in the institution of Australian police custody, such a prerogative of mercy is only momentary. For thereafter the Aboriginal Australian is to be detained in a solitary confinement cell in a correctional facility for up to 22 hours a day.[853]

---

[849] The offence of resisting arrest and/or hindering police in the execution of their duty is prescribed in Section 546C of the *Crimes Act 1900*, and comes with a maximum penalty of 12 months imprisonment and/or an AUD $1,100 fine.

[850] For example, in the Australian Capital Territory, Section 210L of the ACT *Crimes Act 1900*; designates a maximum penalty for this offence is 200 penalty units, imprisonment for 2 years, or both.

[851] Section 60(1) of the *Crimes Act 1900*, makes it an offence punishable by up to 5 years' imprisonment to assault, throw a missile at, stalk, harass, or intimidate a police officer.

[852] On 6 August 1987, Mr. Lloyd James Boney, a 28-year-old Aboriginal man from Brewarrina in northwest New South Wales was violently arrested by three police officers for the breach of his bail conditions. Mr. Boney was found dead 90 minutes later, hanging by a football sock in an Australian police cell. See: Anthony, Thalia. (2016). *Deaths in custody: 25 years after the royal commission, we've gone backwards*. The Conversation. Date accessed: 17 August 2019. Access link: <https://theconversation.com/deaths-in-custody-25-years-after-the-royal-commission-weve-gone-backwards-57109>

In relation to the in police-custody death of Mr. Boney, the Commissioner, J. H. Wootten, in his 1991 report on the gentleman's death found no case of homicide for the police to answer. See: J.H. Wootten. (1991). *Report on the Inquiry into the death of Lloyd James Boney*. Canberra: Australian Govt. Pub. Service.

Aboriginal Elder Mr. Ward suffered third degree burns to his body and was killed, effectively 'cooked to death' in the back of a security van. See: O'Loughlin, Toni. (2009). *Australian Aboriginal prisoner 'cooked to death' in van*. The Guardian. Date accessed: 23 February 2020. Access link: <https://www.theguardian.com/world/2009/jun/14/australia-aborigine-cooked-prison-van>

[853] Sharma, Kriti. (2018). *The Nightmare Lives of Indigenous Prisoners in Australia*. Human Rights Watch. Date accessed: 23 February 2020. Access link: <https://

Such inhumane, unlawful, degrading, and cruel conduct by the Anglo-Saxon police officers of the British Crown, ultimately comes to represent the moral and legal responsibility, not to mention, criminal negligence, of the British Commonwealth of Australia. This horrific treatment of the First Nations Peoples of Australia is tantamount to oppression and torture; a categorical breach of Articles 7 and 10 of the *International Covenant on Civil and Political Rights (1966).*[854]

Furthermore, any just attempt by the Aboriginal people to overthrow the Government of the British Commonwealth, or overthrow the lawful authority of the Government of the British Commonwealth, to rightfully reclaim their sovereignty to Indigenous Country is deemed unlawful conduct. That is to infer, such conduct is tantamount to treachery, pursuant to the *Criminal Code Act 1995 (Cth)*, and consequentially, such [criminal] conduct is punishable by the penalty of imprisonment for life in the British Commonwealth of Australia.[855]

Lest we forget, that this immoral, inhumane, genocidal, and barbaric uncivilised conduct by the white Christian Anglo-Saxon British civilisation occurred in the black Aboriginal people's native country. The Indigenous Australian people's native country, that for the historical record, was attempted to be politically, legally, economically, socially, culturally, and racially reconstructed into

---

www.hrw.org/news/2018/08/09/nightmare-lives-Indigenous-prisoners-australia>

Brull, Michael. (2018). *Behind Bars Part 3: Australia's shocking cruelty to Aboriginal people with disabilities: Solitary confinement.* New Matilda. Date accessed: 23 February 2020. Access link: <https://newmatilda.com/2018/02/19/behind-bars-part-3-australias-shocking-cruelty-aboriginal-people-disabilities-solitary-confinement/>

854 United Nations Human Rights Office of the High Commissioner. (2020). *International Covenant on Civil and Political Rights.* Date accessed: 23 February 2020. Access link: <https://www.ohchr.org/en/professionalinterest/pages/ccpr.aspx>

855 *The Criminal Code Act (Commonwealth) 1995*, Chapter 5, Part 5.1, Division 80, Section 80.1AC, Subsection (c).

the modern white Christian Anglo-Saxon man's country with the advent of the *White Australia Policy* (1901–1973) (see Figure 55) that was enacted with the passage of the *Immigration Restriction Act of 1901 (Cth)*. May God save Her Majesty, the [British] Queen, for it was only a century antecedent that the words inscribed herein were wholly sung throughout the British Commonwealth of Australia:

> *'Australia! Australia!*
> *Sunny South of Old Britannia's sons,*
> *Australia, the white man's land,*
> *Defended by the white man's guns,*
> *Australia! Australia!*
> *For Anglo-Saxon race and Southern Cross,*
> *God Bless and help us to protect*
> *Our glorious land Australia'.*[856]

The Aboriginal Australian people's exercise of self-determination, freedom of association, self-government, freedom of expression, freedom of speech, right to political assembly, exercise of sovereignty, territorial integrity, and independence is perceived as a 'breach of the peace', and the British Commonwealth, State, and Territory Anglo-Saxon police officers must act to preserve their sacred oath to duty, to 'keep and preserve Her Majesty's peace' in the modern British Commonwealth of Australia. Notwithstanding, the modern introduction of the British civilisation in Australia, had there not been an eternal peace for 65,000 years in Australia?

So, who 'breached the peace', who invaded another's sovereign territory? Is there any surprise, that the surviving Aboriginal people perceive foreign relations with the British settlers, or the second Anglo-Saxon Australians, as an exclusive matter of racial prejudice and discrimination? Mr. Roy Jackson, the President of The Indigenous Social Justice Association once claimed that 'as long as the police officers know that they are treated as a protected species by

---

856   Naunton, W.E., and Gyles, H.J.W. (1910). *The Great National Policy Song.*

CHAPTER 6 | HISTORY AND JURISPRUDENCE

Figure 55: The White Australia National Song, 1910.
Image Credit: Museums Victoria (Australia) [Item HT 17014].

their governments, their respective ministers, commissioners, and their fellow officers, that is how they will act".[857] It is an undeniable historical fact that the Federation of Australia was not founded on the British legal doctrine of *Terra Nullius*, however, it was established on occupied Aboriginal land (see Figure 56). Lest we forget.

Figure 56: A Federation-era flag or bunting.
Image Credit: National Museum of Australia. Item Number: 2011.0001.0001.

Fifth, the majority of the surviving constituents of the Aboriginal Australian civilisation have material criminal records against them in the Anglo-Saxon legal system in the modern British Commonwealth of Australia. This is a negative externality that has arisen as a direct consequence of, but not limited to, the following historical factors:

- The British colonisation of Aboriginal Australia

---

857 Korff, Jens. (2019). Aboriginal-police relations. *Creative Spirits*. Date accessed: 30 November 2019. Access link: <https://www.creativespirits.info/aboriginalculture/law/aboriginal-police-relations>

CHAPTER 6 | HISTORY AND JURISPRUDENCE

- Forced Indigenous family separations giving rise to *The Stolen Generations*
- The introduction of Anglo-Saxon and European medication, diseases, drugs, and alcohol
- Institutionalised Aboriginal and Torres Strait Islander child abuse
- A poverty-stricken Aboriginal and Torres Strait Islander people without modern economic prosperity, due to limited employment opportunities, cultural identity loss, loss of sacred land, loss of kinship bonds, loss of distinct racial identity, minimal school education, and systemic racial discrimination in the modern civilised Anglo-Saxon Australian society.
- The dismal socio-economic reality is that the majority of the Aboriginal Australian people work as unskilled labourers, or become dependent upon government welfare assistance programs, if not imprisoned since the age of 10.
- The political repression of the Aboriginal Australian people; the denial of freedom of movement, freedom of assembly and association, freedom of expression, freedom of speech, and the inability to congregate to peacefully protest. All of which collectively function to deprive the Aboriginal Australian people of their autonomy and agency to rightfully assert their lawful claim to the sovereignty of the British Commonwealth of Australia.

These aforementioned factors continue to create social, economic, political, wealth, formal education, personal income, and legal inequality for the Aboriginal civilisation in the British Commonwealth of Australia. Consequently, such contextual factors propel the recourse of the Aboriginal people to petty crimes, alcoholism, drug and substance abuse, sexual assault, child abuse, unplanned pregnancy, domestic violence, and widespread civil disobedience in the conventional Anglo-Saxon Australian society. These destructive criminal acts committed by the Aboriginal people are carried out primarily as forms of resistance to their racial oppression, genocide, and slavery. It is the Aboriginal Australian civilisation's counter-force and real opposition to, the institutionalisation and continued operation of the British civilisations foreign and alien culture, society, language, history, values, religion, legal, political, social, medical, and economic system that is imposed upon the Indigenous Country.

Provisioning proper and due consideration, and in the greater context of the aforementioned factors, the Aboriginal Australian people are the victims of a greater crime. That is to say, the Anglo-Saxon civilisation's crimes of the extermination, genocide, rape, massacre, slavery, and repression of the Indigenous Australian people's inalienable political, civil, legal, cultural, and human rights in the British Commonwealth of Australia.

Sixth, the children of the Aboriginal Australian population are being incarcerated; subjected to arrest and imprisonment, at unprecedented rates, for minor and petty offences against the English common law in the British Commonwealth of Australia, in direct contravention of international humanitarian law; the *United Nations Convention on the Rights of the Child (1989)*.[858] This inhumane solitary detention operates to the major psychological and intellectual detriment of the Aboriginal adolescent, and deprives the Aboriginal children of their fundamental human right to a childhood. Consequently, the Aboriginal children are prevented from achieving a higher education that, in turn, intentionally, contributes towards hindering the development of their full potential and intellectual capacities.

This social reality is counter-intuitive to the development of the successive and future generations of the Aboriginal Australian people, by ensuring that, the Aboriginal Australian people remain unlettered and dependent on the Australian federal government for public housing, public transport, psychological support services,

---

[858] *United Nations Convention on the Rights of the Child (1989).* Article 37, and 40.

CHAPTER 6 | HISTORY AND JURISPRUDENCE

welfare, food, legal counsel, medical and dental care. Ask yourself the vexed question, what future is an Indigenous Australian child going to have, whom at 10 years of age is placed in an Australian prison? What hope is there for the future generation of Aboriginal Australian adults to have a better life than the preceding Indigenous Australian generation in the British Commonwealth of Australia?

Thus, the status quo, the implicit objective of 'Aboriginal civilisation dependency' upon the British Commonwealth of Australia is strengthened. So that the future generations of the Aboriginal Australian people may continue to remain unlettered and incapable of exercising their legal and political 'autonomy', as afforded to them by virtue of *The United Nations Declaration on the Rights of Indigenous Peoples (2007)*. More specifically, in respect to international law, the Aboriginal Australian people's exercise of self-determination, self-government, and the further legal development of their rightful future claims to sovereignty over their rightful territory, duly afforded to the Indigenous population of Australia; the First Nations' Peoples of Country, in accordance with the international treaty law, which gives rise to binding international legal commitments for Australia, have been subject to persistent contravention and violation by this signatory nation-state; the British Commonwealth of Australia.[859, 860, 861, 862]

The establishment of the British Commonwealth of Australia, on behalf of the British Crown, as a modern sovereign nation-state, is founded upon the fictional perception of the Aboriginal people of Australia as a 'dying race'.[863] However, on the contrary, the Aboriginal civilisation was a flourishing civilisation, it became a dying race due to the British civilisation's diseases, genocide,

---

859 *United Nations Declaration on the Rights of Indigenous Peoples (2007)* (A/RES/61/295). Article 3.
860 *United Nations Declaration on the Rights of Indigenous Peoples (2007)*. Article 4.
861 *United Nations Declaration on the Rights of Indigenous Peoples (2007)*. Article 26.
862 On behalf of the Australian Commonwealth, the Rudd Government officially adopted the United Nations Declaration in 2009.
863 McAllister, D. (1878). *The Australian Aboriginies*. Melbourne Review, p. 157.

massacres, slavery, and extermination of the Aboriginal and Torres Strait Islander people in Australia.

The 230-year modern history of the Anglo-Saxon British ancestry convict Australian people and the successive generations of the Anglo-Saxon descent Australian people towards the first Indigenous Australian people has been and continues to be one that is characterised by: arrest the Aboriginal, detain and assault the Aboriginal in police custody, incarcerate the Aboriginal in prison, and kill the Aboriginal, all on native Aboriginal land.

Therefore, it must be thoughtfully inquired as to whether the British Crown's common law; the English common law, is being improperly and immorally employed as an instrument to conduct systematic genocide, racial oppression, slavery, forced institutionalisation, and uphold injustice against the First Nations Peoples of Australia? In any event, what is most apparent in the British Commonwealth of Australia, is that the treatment of the Aboriginal Australian people fundamentally contravenes the tenets of eternal law and natural law.

As a whole, the Australian Indigenous population is the most incarcerated human civilisation on the Earth.[864] The Aboriginal people of the British Commonwealth of Australia have been deprived of their inviolable and fundamental rights to life, land, liberty, and legal equality as recognised by customary international law and enshrined by treaty law in accordance with international law.[865] The vast majority of the Aboriginal Australian people will

---

864 At 30 June 2016, the Aboriginal and Torres Strait Islander imprisonment rate was 2,346 prisoners per 100,000 Aboriginal and Torres Strait Islander population.
As at 30 June 2016, the Aboriginal and Torres Strait Islander prisoner population accounted for 27 per cent of the total Australian prisoner population, this is in the context of the total Aboriginal and Torres Strait Islander population aged 18 years and over representing ca. 2 per cent of the total Australian population aged 18 years and over. See: Australian Bureau of Statistics. (2016). *Aboriginal and Torres Strait Islander Prisoner Characteristics*. 4517.0—Prisoners in Australia, 2016.
865 *United Nations Charter 1945*. Article 1, 55(c), 73(a), and 73(b).
Universal Declaration of Human Rights 1948. Article 1, 2, and 3.

CHAPTER 6 | HISTORY AND JURISPRUDENCE

not achieve marked success in the Anglo-Saxon imposed imperial order; that reeks of the entrenched British economic, legal, historical, religious, social, cultural, and political system in the modern Commonwealth of Australia. In support of this assertion, consider what have the Aboriginal people received in exchange for three centuries of injustice, torture, oppression, incarceration, slavery, racial discrimination, genocide, and deprivation of their natural liberty?

Up to the present time, the Aboriginal Australian people have received three ceremonial retributions, namely:

1. In 1962, the right to vote in Commonwealth and state elections in Australia.[866]
2. In 1992, the High Court's recognition of Aboriginal Native Title claims over Australia.[867]
3. In 2008, a national apology by the Prime Minister of Australia, the Right Honourable Kevin Rudd (r. 2007–2010, and 2013) in the Commonwealth Parliament of Australia, on behalf of the Australian Government.[868]

The most salient of the three aforementioned retributions is point number two on Native Title, which we shall examine further herein. It is imperative to acknowledge that the historical narrative of the High Court's Native Title recognition is considerably intertwined

---

United Nations International Covenant on Civil and Political Rights 1966. Article 21, and 22.
United Nations International Covenant on Economic, Social and Cultural Rights 1966. Article 8(1)(a).
United Nations International Convention on the Elimination of All Forms of Racial Discrimination 1966. Article 5.
United Nations Declaration on the Rights of Indigenous Peoples 2007. Article 3, 4, and 5.

866   Australian Government. (1962). *Commonwealth Electoral Act 1918.*
867   High Court of Australia. (1992). *Mabo v Queensland No. 2* 1992 (Cth).
      Australian Government. (1993). *Native Title Act (Cth).*
868   Australian Government. (2008). *Apology to Australia's Indigenous peoples.* Apology transcript.

with the personal legacy of Edward Koiki Mabo (1936–1992), an Indigenous Australian who was born on Mer (Murray Island). Notwithstanding, Mabo's commitment to the welfare and development of the Aboriginal people in modern Australia, 'Mabo only became concerned with Indigenous land rights when he discovered that Murray Island was British Crown land' under the Australian common law system.[869]

Prior to the High Court's granting of 'special leave' and the determination of the facts relevant to the legal case, the Queensland state legislature specifically sought, by the successful passage of legislative acts of the Queensland state assembly (i.e., *The Queensland Coast Islands Declaratory Act 1985*), to enact statutes for the express purpose of denying the Aboriginal Australian people 'Native Title' claims to their Indigenous country in the Australian state of Queensland, that is, prior to the aforementioned *Mabo v Queensland (No.2) (1992)* case that was heard and ultimately decided by the High Court of Australia.[870]

Subsequent to the landmark legal ruling of the High Court of Australia on 3 June 1992, that consequently gave rise to the initial legislation of the *Native Title Act* being passed in the Australian Parliament in 1993, the original version of the *Native Title Act 1993 (Cth)* legislation has been amended and revised forty-four times since its enactment.

---

[869] National Library of Australia. (2019). *The Mabo Collection*. National Library of Australia. Date accessed: 22 December 2020. Access link: <https://www.nla.gov.au/selected-library-collections/mabo-collection>

[870] The State Parliament of Queensland passed *The Queensland Coast Islands Declaratory Act 1985*, this legislation asserted that, upon being annexed by the Queensland Government in 1879, 'the islands were vested in the British Crown ... freed from all other rights, interests and claims'. This Queensland state legislation served to extinguished, without compensation, any Torres Strait Islander claims to their traditional lands. See: National Archives of Australia. (2020). *Eddie Koiki Mabo and the Mabo Case*. National Archives of Australia. Date accessed: 21 December 2020. Access link: <https://www.naa.gov.au/explore-collection/first-australians/eddie-koiki-mabo-and-mabo-case>

CHAPTER 6 | HISTORY AND JURISPRUDENCE

The fundamental point of distinction and concern herein is that it is not the Aboriginal Australian people in the Federal Parliament of the British Commonwealth of Australia who are exercising their political and legal authority to determine legislative amendments, draft bills, enact revised statutes, and create interpretation acts that will impact their future and entitlement to freehold, not native title, sacred land in their own country; Australia. However, the primary point of importance herein is that the British and European descent immigrants, the second Australians, who are the majority members of the Commonwealth Parliament of Australia, are exercising political power and agency on behalf of the Indigenous Australian people. Where is the political self-determination, self-government, independence, autonomy, and sovereignty for the Indigenous Australian people in the British Commonwealth of Australia? It is non-existent, the Indigenous and Torres Strait Islander people are kept a dependent people, dependent upon the British Commonwealth of Australia.

The British civilisation descent first-fleet alien immigrants, and the subsequent waves of the European, Irish, and Scottish immigrants, not the first and original Indigenous Australian people, exercise the vested political and legal powers to make amendments to restrict, regulate, and govern the operating provisions of the legislation that concerns Indigenous Australian affairs, in order to limit the future sovereignty claims and legal liabilities for the British Commonwealth of Australia, and the British Crown, that may arise from the High Court of Australia's Native Title ruling, through the subsequent legislation enacted by the Federal Parliament of Australia, to effectively govern the strict operation of Native Title or Aboriginal sovereignty claims in the British Commonwealth of Australia. For in legal effect, whilst the High Court's decision in *Mabo v Queensland (No. 2)* [1992] HCA 23, overturned the British Crown's fictitious legal doctrine of *Terra Nullius* (Nobody's Land), however, the High Court of Australia served to safeguard the British assertion of sovereignty in Australia that was established in 1788 as inviolable.

Furthermore, the High Court's judgement also held as lawful, that from that time onwards (i.e., 1788–Present), there was, politically and legally, only one sovereign power (i.e., the British Crown), and one legal system of positive law (i.e., the English Common Law) operable in the British Commonwealth of Australia. Thereby, nullifying, attempting to wholly extinguish, the Aboriginal Australian people's rightful territorial claims to the entire British Commonwealth of Australia along with the operation of customary Aboriginal law in the British Commonwealth of Australia.

For the High Court of Australia knew, or at the very least, ought to have known, that had it determined otherwise, had it decided otherwise, the entire legal, political, historical, economic, cultural, and social basis of the modern British Commonwealth of Australia would have been declared null and void. And if that had become the case, what would have happened to the all the non-Indigenous Australians in the British Commonwealth of Australia? Perhaps they would have be declared as *de jure* stateless people.[871] Notwithstanding the pyrrhic nature of the legal victory to the Australian Aboriginal people, the significance of the High Court's 1992 Mabo legal ruling resides in the establishment of *Aboriginal sovereignty* over the *British Commonwealth* of Australia. What was previously a *historical* fact, has now, after 204 years, been recognised as a contemporary *legal* fact.

It is an irrefutable and indisputable fact, without qualification or modification whatsoever, that if the fictitious founding British doctrine of the Commonwealth of Australia (i.e., *Terra Nullius*) has been legally repealed. Then on what doctrine, ideology, principle, basis, or foundation does the Anglo-Saxon sovereignty rest? None, period. Therefore, Aboriginal Sovereignty was never ceded to the British Crown from the Indigenous Australian people. In

---

871   *The Convention Relating to the Status of Stateless Persons 1954, Article 1(1).*

addition, there is no founding treaty of the British Commonwealth of Australia between the Indigenous people and the British Crown, that affirms the lawful and perpetual transfer of sovereignty to the British Crown, in order, that the British Crown may lawfully give rise to the formation, the existence, of the British Commonwealth of Australia.

On the contrary, the Anglo-Saxon British descent immigrants, the second Australians, are unlawfully situated on the occupied sovereign territory of the oppressed and incarcerated Aboriginal Australian people! Had the High Court of Australia so recognised, so affirmed this self-evident and inalienable truth of the immoral dispossession of Aboriginal sacred land, not to mention, the genocide, the slavery, the incarceration, the cultural destruction, the forced removal of Aboriginal children from their parents, the rape, the massacres, and the racial oppression of the Aboriginal Australian people, it would have effectuated into motion the existential demise of the body politic of the British Commonwealth of Australia. The rightful reclamation of sovereignty to the Aboriginal Australian people is constantly obstructed, a miscarriage of justice, an obstruction of natural justice transpired in the High Court's ruling on the Mabo case. Here is the fundamental 'breach of the peace' in the British Commonwealth of Australia. Lest we forget.

Notwithstanding, the limitations of the High Court's determination on the existence of Native Title, the current compilation of the *Native Title Act*, in force, protects and grants immunity to the position of the British Crown with respect to legal prosecution arising from prospective Aboriginal people's native title land claims and legal proceedings for the redress of any historical acts that could be legally proven to have been committed that were detrimental, or perceived as having a detrimental effect, to the Aboriginal Australian civilisation, by the Anglo-Saxon colonial representatives of the British Crown.[872]

---

872 In order for a valid claim to traditional land under the Australian Native Title

The *Native Title Act*, Part 1, Section 4, Subsection 5, explicitly states:

'This Act binds the Crown in right of the Commonwealth, of each of the States, of the Australian Capital Territory and of the Northern Territory. However, nothing in this Act renders the Crown liable to be prosecuted for an offence.'[873]

For in the British common law system, there exist two primary sources for the creation of positive law: Judge-made case law (i.e., legal rulings by magistrates, justices, and the chief justice in a court of law), and legislation (i.e., acts and statutes of the federal, state, and territory parliaments by senators and ministers). Given that there existed (no favourable) legislative or body of case law precedent to the HCA Native Title legal ruling on the Mabo case, in this instance, the Australian common law evolved subject to the case law method.[874] Notwithstanding that the legal precedent of the Native Title that was established by the High Court pursuant to the Mabo case, under the English common law system, the High Court of Australia must interpret and apply the law, as created by the legislature (i.e., the Commonwealth/ the Federal Parliament). That

---

law regime, the Indigenous Australian people must be able to demonstrate the following:

First, the continued possession of rights and interests under the traditional laws currently acknowledged and the traditional customs currently observed. Those laws and customs must have been acknowledged and passed down from generation to generation from the the time of British settlement until the present time; and

Second, demonstrate a continued connection with the land in question by the traditional laws and ancient customs.

873 Australian Government. (1993). *Native Title Act (Cth) 1993.* Part 1, Section 4, Subsection 5.

874 This would not have been possible prior to the enactment of the *Australia Act 1986,* which conferred upon Australia the status of a 'sovereign, independent, and federal nation'. For prior to 1986, the British legal system would have had the final legal authority to make the highest decisions and was the final legal recourse to appeal (i.e., the Privy Council), thus, the British would never have overturned their own legal principle of *terra nullius* as the legal foundation of the Commonwealth of Australia.

is to infer, in a representative democracy, and a sovereign nation-state with a responsible government such as the Commonwealth of Australia, the purpose of the common law courts is to 'give effect to the will of Parliament'.[875]

Furthermore, given that the Federal Parliament of Australia has, consequent to the High Court's Mabo case ruling, enacted the *Native Title Act 1993* legislation and passed forty-four amendments to it, all future native title claims must now be considered by any Australian court of law (i.e., state, territory, federal, or the High Court of Australia) in the legal context, in accordance with the operable legislation in force in the Commonwealth of Australia. This serves to confine and restrict the purview of the Australian Courts in their independent judicial assessment of native title claims to the contemporary legal interpretation of the *Native Title Act 1993 No. 110, 1993, Compilation No. 44*, in force from 29 December 2018, until a subsequent compilation amendment of the Native Title Act is passed by the Federal Parliament of Australia.

The force of positive law is being employed in a deliberate and intentional manner by the Federal Parliament of Australia, and the elected members of that sovereign Commonwealth Parliament, who are predominantly British and European in their ancestry, in order to alter the trajectory of the development and claims arising from the Native Title law that impact the Aboriginal and Torres Strait Islander people's connection to Indigenous Country, by the exercise of constitutional powers conferred upon the sovereign Federal Parliament of Australia to create and repeal laws. In effect, legislation which the Australian law courts must accede to in their legal determinations concerning civil and criminal proceedings within the territory and jurisdiction of the sovereign Commonwealth of Australia.

---

875 In *Al-Kateb v Godwin* [2004] HCA 37 n 19, Gleeson CJ stated: '... [the] principle of legality ... governs both Parliament and the courts. In exercising their judicial function, courts seek to give effect to the will of Parliament by declaring the meaning of what Parliament has enacted.

For the recognition of Native Title may have partially redressed a historical wrong of the British civilisation in modern Australia, however, Indigenous land rights are subject to the jurisdiction of the Australian common law. Therefore, the Aboriginal Australian people have part of their native land returned to them, subject to the caveat, that the English Common law applies to its recognition, regulation, and function in the British Commonwealth of Australia. According to the *Australian Trade and Investment Commission*, as of 2015 Native Title has been recognised over 2,469,647 km² (or ca. 32 per cent) upon the territory of the British Commonwealth of Australia.[876] Furthermore, the *National Native Title Tribunal* evidences that the majority of the Native Title claims are situated in Western Australia, South Australia, Queensland, and the Northern Territory.[877]

One must critically examine, does the English common law operate in a just, equitable, and fair manner for the Indigenous Australian people in the British Commonwealth of Australia? Or is it a mechanism, an instrument, for the British civilisation to impose its will, its English way of life, its culture, its history, its institutions, its socio-economic principles, its authority and rules, upon the Australian Aboriginal civilisation, for the ulterior motive of the immoral and unjust oppression of the Indigenous Australian people? For ultimately, that is the salient question to fathom herein.

The British, European, Irish, and Scottish descent Australian people possess the legal authority and the right honourable standing in the Australian Federal Parliament to enact statutes, legislation, and acts of parliament, to govern the Aboriginal people's legal standing in the contemporary Australian society; Aboriginal land,

---

876 Australian Trade and Investment Commission. (2020). *Native Title*. Australian Trade and Investment Commission. Date accessed: 22 December 2020. Access link: <https://www.austrade.gov.au/land-tenure/Native-title/native-title>

877 James Cook University Australia. (2020). *Eddie Koiki Mabo Timeline*. James Cook University Australia. Date accessed: 22 December 2020. Access link: <https://libguides.jcu.edu.au/mabo-timeline/2020>

social, cultural, civil, political, and human rights and more generally, the governance of their daily life. The Aboriginal people have been forced into the inferior condition of a dependent civilisation; a civilisation that is institutionalised, and has been deprived of self-determination, personal agency, human dignity, natural liberty, and human freedom of expression in their own country.

For it is not, the Aboriginal and Torres Strait Islander people, collectively the First Australians, that, as a collective majority, stand as the elected representatives of their community and people in the Australian State, Territory, and Federal Parliaments, to exercise their own independent vested political agency and engage in political discourse during discussion time, reading time, the tabling of motions and bills, the voting on proposed legislation, and determining the enactment and passage of bills at sitting sessions within the State, Territory, and Federal Parliaments of the Commonwealth of Australia.

Rather, the Aboriginal people have been deprived of civil and political engagement, human agency, self-determination in the parliamentary political process, but are nonetheless subject to its outcomes; the federal, state, and territorial laws, acts, and statutes of the parliaments within the lawful jurisdiction and territory of the Commonwealth of Australia. This conduct is tantamount to a direct infraction of the international law; the *United Nations Declaration on the Rights of Indigenous Peoples (2007)*.[878]

In the political-legal affirmation of this international instrument (i.e., UNDRIP 2007), only four of the United Nations Member States; the four Commonwealth Bible Countries, voted against its adoption at the United Nations General Assembly in 2007.[879] The very concept of democracy, as a political form of governance, is materially non-existent and continues to be denied, for the Aboriginal

---

[878] *United Nations Declaration on the Rights of Indigenous Peoples (2007)*. Article 18, 19, and 20(1).

[879] The Commonwealth of Australia, Canada, New Zealand, and the United States of America.

and Torres Strait Islander peoples of the British Commonwealth of Australia.

Politically, a democracy represents 'rule by the many', or 'rule by the people', or it can constitute a 'tyranny of the majority'.[880] The limitations and flaws of democratic political organisation are omnipresent, as recognised by the British Prime Minister Winston Churchill (1874–1965), 'no one pretends that democracy is perfect or all-wise. Indeed, it has been said that democracy is the worst form of government except for all of the other forms which have been tried from time to time'.[881]

Now in the particular case of the Australian Aboriginal and Torres Strait Islander people, how can the minority of the Aboriginal and Torres Strait Islander people be inferred to exercise their inalienable political rights through a democratic form of civil government in Australia? Even with the proper legal and political-institutional affirmation of their 'right to vote' in the late twentieth century in Australia, for the two Indigenous Australian civilisations that, in the twenty-first century, collectively, constitute less than five per cent of the total Australian national population.[882]

Presuming that in 1219, the Aboriginal and Torres Strait Islander people in Australia would have represented ca. 95 per cent of the continental population; the majority has now become the minority, through the employment of the British civilisation's genocide, colonisation, and settlement over three successive centuries. Upon the British civilisation's genocide of the Indigenous Australian people, how politically convenient that *The Convention*

---

880 Madison, James. (1788). *Federalist Papers*. No. 51 in: Hamilton, A., Madison, J., and Jay, J. (2015). *The Federalist Papers: A Collection of Essays Written in Favour of the New Constitution*. Ohio: Coventry House Publishing, p. 98.

881 UK Parliament. (1947). *Parliament Bill: HC Deb 11 November 1947, Volume 444, cc 203–321*. United Kingdom Parliament. Date accessed: 10 May 2020. Access link: <https://api.parliament.uk/historic-hansard/commons/1947/nov/11/parliament-bill>

882 Australian Bureau of Statistics. (2016). *The 2016 Census of Population and Housing*.

on the *Prevention and Punishment of the Crime of Genocide (1948)* came into force in the mid-twentieth century, when the immoral, inhumane, and unconscionable conduct of the British civilisation was more or less complete, throughout the modern civilised world, but for the failed particular case of the Union of South Africa, which did not wholly materialise into a Bible Commonwealth nation-state.

How can the Aboriginal and Torres Strait Islander Australian people ever be in a majority position to represent a sufficient proportion of the population of Australian citizens, in order to secure the 'majority vote' to ensure greater Indigenous Australian people's democratic representation in the Australian Federal Parliament? Even if the entire Aboriginal population, ca. four percent of the nation-state's population, across Australia voted in the relevant state, territory, and federal general elections, they will never be in a political position to possess, at any given point in time in the next hundred years, the majority number of the available senator seats that are held by the elected representatives to each state, territory, and federal parliament in the British Commonwealth of Australia.[883]

The grand question then becomes, given the dire exigency of the contemporary political situation, how does one propose to eliminate the institutionalised inequality in political representation and legal access for the Aboriginal and Torres Strait Islander Australian people in the British Commonwealth of Australia?

The *United Nations Declaration on the Rights of Indigenous Peoples*, Article 18, asserts that:

'Indigenous peoples have the right to participate in decision-making in matters which would affect their rights, through

---

883   According the Australian Bureau of Statistics, in 2016, the Aboriginal and Torres Strait Islander Australians represent 3.3 per cent of the total Australian population, or 798,365 people. See: Australian Bureau of Statistics. (2018). *Estimates of Aboriginal and Torres Strait Islander Australians.* Australian Bureau of Statistics. Date accessed: 21 December 2020. Access link: <https://www.abs.gov.au/statistics/people/aboriginal-and-torres-strait-islander-peoples/estimates-aboriginal-and-torres-strait-islander-australians/latest-release>

representatives chosen by themselves in accordance with their own procedures, as well as to maintain and develop their own Indigenous decision-making institutions.'[884]

The aforementioned United Nations Declaratory Right, provided for by international treaty law, cannot be achieved, subject to the exclusive parameters of the existing legal and political structures in force in the British Commonwealth of Australia. In effect, the status quo Anglo-Saxon institutions and legal-political structures represent a fundamental impediment to the progress of the Aboriginal and Torres Strait Islander Australian people's legal, civil, human, cultural, and political rights; self-determination, self-government, and the exercise of lawful sovereignty over wholly Aboriginal native land, that the British Commonwealth of Australia unlawfully occupies through the enactment, enforcement, and empowerment of the common law, the police force, and the military's armed forces.

Having examined the historical realities and the broader contemporary nature of the seemingly intractable problem of bilateral relations between the Indigenous Australian people and the British Australian people. This latter section of the thesis proposes a relevant resolution to the inequity that the Aboriginal Australian people confront in the British Commonwealth of Australia. The only complete and irreversible method to secure genuine reconciliation is to be effectuated on the four founding principles of the 'Reconciliation Action Plan':

1. The establishment of the First Australians Indigenous People's Parliament, parallel and concurrent to the Commonwealth Parliament of Australia;
2. The resumption of the operation of Aboriginal customary and traditional laws, parallel and concurrent to the Commonwealth of Australia's Federal, State, and Territory laws;

---

[884] *United Nations Declaration on the Rights of Indigenous Peoples.* (2007). A/61/295. Article 18.

3. The establishment of Aboriginal law courts and a customary law legal system, parallel and concurrent to the Commonwealth, State, and Territory Australian law courts, and the English common law legal system; and
4. The establishment of an Aboriginal Police Force, parallel and concurrent to the Commonwealth, State, and Territory Australian Police Forces.

This proposed four-point 'Reconciliation Action Plan' aims to achieve the *restoration of sovereignty* for the Aboriginal Australian people through a dual and shared sovereignty model, and it is exclusively restricted in its application to the internal affairs of the Commonwealth of Australia, and in governing the Aboriginal-Commonwealth bilateral relations.

The Aboriginal people did not engage in foreign relations outside of Australia prior to 1788, and thus, there is no miscarriage, or denial, of social justice in the event that the Commonwealth of Australia, on behalf of the British Crown, retains the exclusive legal right to the governance of foreign affairs and political recognition as the sole legitimate government of Australia by the International Community of sovereign nation-states and the numerous international institutions with demonstrable and distinct international legal personality in the contemporary modern civilised world.[885]

In effect, the British Crown ought to, retrospectively, recognise the applicability of the international legal principle of suzerainty as true and valid in 1788 within Australia. That is a dominant sovereign nation-state, Great Britain, controlling the foreign relations of a vassal state, Indigenous Australia. However, now the British Crown ought to wholly permit the Indigenous Australian people to exercise

---

885 The United Nations its special agencies and associated organisations: the World Trade Organisation, the International Labour Organisation, the International Monetary Fund, the Organisation for Economic Co-operation and Development, the World Bank, and the World Health Organisation.

dual and shared sovereign authority in Australia's internal affairs that are, and remain, in so far as relevant to the Aboriginal and Torres Strait Islander people's legal, social, economic, and political governance of their Indigenous Country.

For the contemporary state of foreign relations in the modern civilised world, represents an innovation in the International Relations of Australia with the rest of the modern civilised world, post-colonisation, post-1788, and therefore, the Aboriginal and Torres Strait Islander people are not denied their historical heritage-based political, cultural, moral, civil, economic, and legal rights to self-determination, self-government, and sovereignty over the internal Aboriginal affairs and sacred Indigenous land, as was existent prior to the introduction of the British civilisation in Australia.

In practical effect, the Aboriginal and Torres Strait Islander people cannot be inferred to have relinquished or lost any legal or political rights that they did not possess or exercise during their exclusive inhabitancy of the territory of Australia. That is to infer, the Aboriginal and Torres Strait Islander people do not possess a legal claim, by extension of their original inhabitancy of the land of Australia, to the governance of foreign relations, international commerce, bilateral and multilateral treaties, international agreements, and nation-state membership to the international institutions, that did not exist prior to 1788. As such, the contemporary inter-governmental functions of the International Relations that did not exist as part and parcel of the Indigenous Australian civilisation, shall lawfully remain vested and rightfully institutionalised in the British Commonwealth of Australia.

The globalisation of the International Community of sovereign and independent nation-states is predominantly a modern construct of the Western civilisation, a political-legal-social-economic-technological development of the modern civilised world (i.e., the *universal establishment* of sovereign republics, foreign embassies, international diplomacy, bilateral and multilateral relationships amongst sovereign and independent nation-states, inter-governmental organisations, international institutions, international civil society, and non-government organisations).

In this context, constitutional powers in relation to foreign relations, international treaties, foreign commerce, defence, and other external affairs related matters shall remain vested within the exclusive jurisdiction and purview of the Commonwealth of Australia, its established democratic and civil government, parliament, common law courts, defence force, and other relevant institutions.[886]

However, internally within the Commonwealth of Australia, for the Aboriginal and Torres Strait Islander citizens; the Aboriginal Parliament, Indigenous customary laws, traditional courts, legal system and police force shall represent the highest legal authority and political governance for the Indigenous subjects, and their operable legal jurisdiction is constricted for the exclusive application of the Aboriginal and Torres Strait Islander people only. That is to infer, the Aboriginal and Torres Strait Islander people are not subjects of the British Crown. Recognising and affording the Aboriginal and Torres Strait Islander people a historical legal right, an inviolable sovereign right that they have held uninterrupted for circa. 65,000 years prior to the advent of the British civilisation's colonisation of modern Australia.[887]

With the significant historical event of the British civilisation's discovery of the continent of Australia by Lieutenant James Cook in 1770, originally, the modern history falsely recorded the continent of Australia to be founded upon the legal doctrine of *Terra Nullius* (Nobody's Land). Notwithstanding this fictional British claim, originally the application of English common law was never intended to be applied to the Aboriginal and Torres Strait Islander

---

886 Commonwealth of Australia. (2003). *Commonwealth of Australia Constitution Act*. Part V, Section 51 (xxix).
887 Clarkson, Chris., and Jacobs, Zenobia et. al. (2017). Human occupation of northern Australia by 65,000 years ago. *Nature*. 547, (20 July 2017), pp. 306–310.

subjects in Australia.[888] This is a historical and legal founding fact initially recognised in the Constitution of Australia.[889] Therefore, the political and legal solution proposed herein serves as a legal remedy to prospectively rectify the injustices of the British Crown against the Indigenous Australian people in the contemporary modern foundation of the body politic of the British Commonwealth of Australia.

The proposed legal and political iteration of Australia will result in the establishment of a two-tier political-legal system of governing parliaments and laws that are both concurrently equal and valid within the one sovereign nation-state. The emergence of this 'dual sovereignty' model will aspire to justly resolve the historical injustices of the past committed by, and in the name of, the British Crown, and thereby, foster the prevalence of an eternal and natural justice in the Commonwealth of Australia. This Reconciliation Action Plan is proposed as a full and final settlement on the complex issue of the Aboriginal and Torres Strait Islander Australian people's equitable reconciliation to Indigenous Country.

It cannot be held, nor purported, that the Aboriginal and Torres Strait Islander people will achieve the same level of recognition and equivalent treatment, in a contemporary political and legal governance system that is fundamentally established upon an alien

---

888 'But this must be understood with very many and very great restrictions. Such colonists carry with them only so much of the English law as is applicable to their new situation and the condition of an infant colony.' See: Blackstone, William. (R. Burn, and J. Williams, Eds.) (1791). *Commentaries on the Laws of England*. Volume I, p. 108.

889 The Commonwealth Parliament was denied power to make laws with respect to people of 'the aboriginal race in any State'. Section 51(xxvi) of the Constitution, conferred on Parliament the power to make laws with respect to 'the people of any race, other than the aboriginal race in any State, for whom it is deemed necessary to make special laws.'
In addition, Section 127 of the Constitution provided: 'In reckoning the numbers of the people of the Commonwealth, or of a State or other part of the Commonwealth, aboriginal natives shall not be counted.' See: Pritchard, Sarah. (2011). The 'Race' Power in Section 51(XXVI) of the Constitution. *Australian Indigenous Law Review*. Volume 15, No. 2, p. 45.

and foreign British civilisations' ideals, positive laws, language, culture, history, institutions, traditions, customs, society, morals, religion, lifestyle, and principles, to those of the Aboriginal people's ancient customary practices, heritage, traditional laws, and sacred traditions. A just and eternal peace in accordance with eternal law must be established upon the premise of 'one country—two equal systems' in the Commonwealth of Australia.

This thesis acknowledges that this proposal may never effectuate to become a conventional reality in the twenty-first-century Australia. However, this is the most reasonable and equitable option for the shared future prosperity of the *First Indigenous* Australians and the *Second British* ancestry Australians, in Country and Commonwealth, respectively. Genuine reconciliation can only ever be realised through *acta, non verba* (deeds, not words).

The reader will take note that *this reconciliation proposal has not endorsed constitutional recognition* for the Indigenous Australian people. *Nor has this reconciliation proposal endorsed the concept of a legal and binding treaty* between the First Nations People of Australia and the British Commonwealth of Australia. This thesis expresses the perspective that these belated symbolic artefacts are most representative of tokenism, and will achieve little of practical significance or real immediate worth in genuinely resolving the past injustices committed against the Aboriginal and Torres Strait Islander Australian people by the British civilisation, in the name of the British Crown. The time for a founding treaty of Australia has elapsed, and it will now only serve to recognise what is a whole imbalance of political, social, economic, cultural, civil, and legal power between the Indigenous Australian people, and the British, European, Irish, and Scottish ancestry Australians in the Commonwealth of Australia.

Furthermore, it is this thesis' perspective, that if a legal treaty was ever to be formalised and ratified, it should be between the First Nations People of Australia and the British Crown (not the Commonwealth of Australia, although it may be a signatory party to such a founding treaty). For ultimately the initial interaction upon invasion, conquest, genocide, slavery, colonisation, and settlement was between the representatives of the British Crown and the Indigenous Australian people.

However, the passage of the *Australia Act 1986* by the Commonwealth Parliament of Australia and the Sovereign Parliament of the United Kingdom has complicated legal endeavours for the British Crown to now enact such a binding and legal treaty between the Indigenous Australian people and the British Crown on the sovereign territory of the Commonwealth of Australia. For the aforementioned Australia Act severed the operable constitutional linkages with Great Britain; relations with the British Parliament, the British Judiciary, and the Privy Council.

Consequently, in the contemporary legal context, only Australia's relations with the British Crown remain intact, which may also be severed in the future, however, at the present time of writing this 'Reconciliation Action Plan' they are not severed. That is to infer, if a future referendum was proposed to the Australian people, and they positively affirmed the creation of the Republic of Australia, then, the final relationship to the British Crown will be irreversibly severed, and the genesis of an independent and sovereign nation-state of Australia shall arise, whereupon His Majesty the King or Her Majesty the Queen of the United Kingdom of Great Britain and Northern Ireland, shall thereafter no longer be the Royal Head of State of the Commonwealth of Australia.

Thus, at present, the exclusive plausible remedy, in the event that a founding treaty is sought between the Indigenous Australian people and the British Crown, is for the British Queen of the United Kingdom of Great Britain and Northern Ireland, Her Majesty Queen Elizabeth II, in her royal capacity, as the Sovereign and Lawful Head of the Commonwealth of Australia, to exercise her vested royal powers and directly effectuate a lawful treaty with the Indigenous people of Australia, which shall have the force of law in the Commonwealth of Australia, and can be subsequently ratified thereafter by the Federal Parliament of Australia.

Once again, this thesis perceives the legal treaty measure of greater symbolic value and historical significance, and rather than focus on the semantics and syntax of treaty-formation, this 'Reconciliation Action Plan' has opted for the practical pursuit of the more constructive and immediate measures that can create a profound effect on the lives of the Indigenous Australian people in the present generation. As an ancient and modern Australian nation-state, let us now forever '*close the gap*' on the basis of truth, equity, and justice between the Indigenous Australian people and the non-Indigenous Australian people.[890]

993

On the principle of social justice. When we seek the deliverance of social justice in the presence of the law courts of a sovereign nation-state, within an adversarial legal system, the adversarial party with more considerable resources at its disposal is more likely than not to be situated in an advantageous position to further promote its legal case and argument in a more sophisticated manner, regardless of the merits of the case. Consequently, the more resourceful party increases its likelihood of securing a favourable legal judgement (verdict) unto its particular position, against the opposing party vis-à-vis a court of law.

Social justice, as the highest ideal that the human civilisation can aspire to, must not be about 'deep pockets' of constituents in

---

890 Department of the Prime Minister and Cabinet. (2019). *Closing the Gap Report 2019*. Department of the Prime Minister and Cabinet. Date accessed: 21 December 2020. Access link: <https://www.niaa.gov.au/sites/default/files/reports/closing-the-gap-2019/index.html>
National Indigenous Australians Agency. (2020). *Closing the Gap: National Agreement on Closing the Gap*. National Indigenous Australians Agency. Date accessed: 21 December 2020. Access link: <https://www.niaa.gov.au/indigenous-affairs/closing-gap>

the conventional society. Rather, the legal system of a sovereign nation-state ought to constitute an accessible mechanism for the achievement of a fair, just, and equitable outcome, exclusively with regard to the facts of the legal case. The most noble and honourable ideals for humanity to aspire towards; social justice and transcendental truth are accordant, you cannot have the presence of social justice, in the absence of transcendental truth, or vice-versa. Regrettably, the perdurable words of Cornelius Tacitus of Rome (56 AD – 120 AD), 'Sorrows are continually the lot of the good, happiness of the wicked', seem to ring truer than ever in the twenty-first century modern civilised world, in particular when it comes to the universal access of social justice in the law courts of a sovereign and independent nation-state.[891]

994

The ancient church religious dogmatic doctrine and the modern sovereign nation-state engineered secular political ideology can both become prodigious impediments to the progress of the human civilisation; a detriment to the universal material, cultural, literary, scientific, artistic, and intellectual progress of humanity, writ large. In relation to the former impediment, historically, consider the unquestioned rule of *Catholicism*; the Roman Catholic Church's social, political, cultural, economic, military, and legal hold of power over the unenlightened and unlettered masses across the continent of Europe. It is not a hyperbole to assert that the progress of the European civilisation was at a standstill for ca. 900 years during the dark Middle Ages, i.e., from the fifth century to the fourteenth century.

For it was the beginning of the *European Renaissance*, at the commencement of the fourteenth century, that marked the turning

---

891   Cornelius Tacitus. (Alfred John Church, William Jackson Brodribb, and Sara Bryant., Eds.) (1942). *The Annals*. New York: Random House, Inc., Book VI, Chapter XXII.

point of an unparalleled period of human advancement in the Western civilisation within the natural sciences (i.e., Brahe, Bruno, Copernicus, Galileo, Kepler (see Figure 57), Leibniz, and Newton), natural philosophy (i.e., Francis Bacon, Berkeley, Campanella, Descartes, Hobbes, Hume, Kant, Locke, Mirandola, Nietzsche, Spinoza (see Figure 58), and Schopenhauer), liberal arts (i.e., Machiavelli's The Prince), classical literature (i.e., Dante's Divine Comedy), classical music (i.e., Bach, Beethoven, Haydn, Mozart, and Vivaldi), famous artworks and paintings (i.e., da Vinci, Caravaggio, Raphael, and Michelangelo), and avant-garde dramatic plays (i.e., Shakespeare).

Not to mention, the subsequent cumulative advent of the *Age of Discovery* in the fifteenth century, which established the modern basis for the global dominance of the Western civilisation across the physical world. In fact, some of the greatest historical artworks in the modern history of the Western civilisation were created during the European Renaissance period, and are attributed to the artistic genius of Michelangelo, such as the *Statue of David*, the *Sistine Chapel Ceiling*, and the *Last Judgement*.

The *European Renaissance* epoch marked the transition period from the *Middle Ages* to *Modernity*. The elevation of human reason, the greater utility of the scientific method, the greater primacy of empiricism and positivism in the governance of the human understanding of the physical world, and a greater 'mathematical' perspective on the observable Universe.

The genius minds of Boyle, Brahe (see Figure 59), Bruno, Copernicus, Descartes, Galileo, Herschel, Kepler, Leibniz, Mariotte, and Newton circumvented the religious indoctrination and theological dogma associated with the Catholic faith, and these select individuals ultimately contributed to the establishment of the modern foundation of secular human scientific knowledge with Sir Isaac Newton's Three Scientific Laws, whom himself was a beneficiary of his predecessors intellectual groundwork; including, but not limited to, René Descartes' Mechanistic Philosophy,

Figure 57: The German astronomer and mathematician Johannes Kepler.
Image Credit: Science Museum / Science & Society Picture Library.

CHAPTER 6 | HISTORY AND JURISPRUDENCE

Figure 58: The Dutch philosopher Baruch Spinoza.
Image Credit: Granger Historical Picture Archive / Alamy.

Figure 59: The Danish astronomer and mathematician Tycho Brahe.
Image Credit: The Royal Observatory, Edinburgh / Science Photo Library.

Johannes Kepler's Laws of Planetary Motion, and Galileo Galilei's Laws of Terrestrial Motion.[892, 893] Notwithstanding, Sir Isaac Newton (1643-1727) also happened to engage in scientific inquiry, in a more progressive and liberal modern era that was considerably more tolerant of his grand scientific experimental endeavours and intellectual writings, than four hundred years antecedent.[894]

On the totality of death and destruction caused by radical ideology during the twentieth century international politics. In relation to the modern sovereign nation-state's enactment of secular and radical political ideology, consider the particular incidence of the nation-state enacted propaganda and ideology in the particular cases of the Union of Soviet Socialist Republics, the People's Republic of China, and Hitler's *Third Reich* of the NAZI Germany. In the Soviet Union's case, Vladimir Lenin (r. 1922-1924) employed Karl Marx's communist and socialist ideology, in connexion with Lenin's own variant of radical left-wing Communism, to create an entirely new sovereign nation-state apparatus; a Soviet nation-state in 1922 that was modelled on the novel fundamental ideology of Marxism-Leninism.

Following the death of the Soviet Premier Lenin, he was succeeded by Joseph Stalin (r. 1924-1953). It was predominantly during the dark period of the Soviet Premier Stalin's tenure, 'that no

---

892 Sir Isaac Newton's Three Scientific Laws:
   1. Every object in a state of uniform motion will remain in that state of motion unless an external force act upon it.
   2. Force equals mass times acceleration.
   3. For every action, there is an equal and opposite reaction.
893 Sir Isaac Newton (1643-1727) 'If I have seen further than others, it is by standing upon the shoulders of giants.' See: Poston, G. J. (2008). Standing on the shoulders of giants. *European Journal of Surgical Oncology*. Volume 34, p. 254.
894 Alexander Pope (1688-1744) 'Nature, and Nature's Laws lay hid in Night. God said, Let Newton be! and All was Light.' See: Alexander Pope. (J. Warton, Ed.) (1822). *The Works of Alexander Pope*. London: J. F. Dove and Richard Priestly, p. 379.

fewer than 20 million Soviet citizens were put to death by the Soviet regime, or died as a direct result of its repressive policies'.[895]

In China's case, Chairman Mao's communist and socialist political ideology; a variant of Marxism-Leninism, namely Maoism, established the ideological basis for the People's Republic of China (est. 1949). Chairman Mao's enactment of public (national state) policy of the *Great Leap Forward* (1958–1962) and the *Cultural Revolution* (1966–1976); both political initiatives that amounted to colossal public policy failures, resulted in the deaths of at least ca. 30 million Chinese citizens in the twentieth century.[896] In addition, the radical and fundamental NAZI ideology of the German *Third Reich* (i.e., Nazism) institutionalised by *Führer* Adolf Hitler, served to ensure the demise of ca. six million innocent Jewish people across the European continent during the course of *World War II* (1939–1945).[897]

995

On sexism as it relates to the cannon of the Anglo-Saxon civilisation's common law. Within the sacred institution of marriage, when domestic violence results in an physical altercation between the husband and wife, and in the heat of the moment, if the husband proceeds to murder his wife, he may determine to have the matter proceed to a criminal trial by jury, on the legal presumption that he plead 'not guilty' to the charge of 'voluntary manslaughter'.

---

895 Satter, David. (2017). *100 Years of Communism—and 100 Million Dead*. Wall Street Journal. Date accessed: 23 October 2020. Access link: <https://www.wsj.com/articles/100-years-of-communismand-100-million-dead-1510011810>

896 Smil, Vaclav. (1999). China's Great Famine: 40 Years Later. *British Medical Journal*. Volume 319, p. 1619.

897 U.S. Holocaust Memorial Museum. (2019). *Documenting Numbers of Victims of the Holocaust and Nazi Persecution*. U.S. Holocaust Memorial Museum. Date accessed: 15 June 2019. Access link: <https://encyclopedia.ushmm.org/content/en/article/documenting-numbers-of-victims-of-the-holocaust-and-nazi-persecution>

The husband's legal defence is that this alleged crime was due to the 'heat of passion'.[898]

Now in a direct physical confrontation, generally speaking, in most cases, the female sex is unlikely to transcend the male sex through the application of brute and lethal force. Therefore, a wife will not be in the prime position, she will be more unlikely than likely that is, to murder her husband in a physical domestic violence altercation, and consequently, the female sex will not be provisioned with the opportunity to plead 'guilty' or 'not guilty' to the lesser criminal charge of voluntary manslaughter in a court of law.

Now for the purpose of our legal analysis assume, if the woman chooses to retreat in the heat of a domestic argument or the husband-wife physical altercation, then subsequently, she plans to murder her husband at a later date, at a more opportune moment, when her spouse would be most vulnerable, or be subject to the tact of surprise (i.e., when her husband is asleep). In this instance, if the female sex were to plead guilty, the female sex would most likely have to plead guilty to the higher criminal charge of first-degree murder; due to the premeditated intention of murder having been effectuated.[899] The perceived quality of human thought underwriting the female's criminal act and her intentional, rational, and planned psychological response to her immediate and personal abuse from domestic violence is perceived as a greater crime at common law within the sovereign nation-state. This latter lethal 'premeditated' response of the female sex is, in the deliverance of justice at common law, a criminal act of greater severity in its crime, than that of the husband killing his wife in the heat of passion and uncontrollable emotional rage.

---

898 Dressler, Joshua. (1982). Rethinking Heat of Passion: A Defence in Search of a Rationale. *The Journal of Criminal Law and Criminology.* Volume 73, No. 2, (Summer, 1982), pp. 421–470.
899 Perkins, Rollin M. (1934). A Re-Examination of Malice Aforethought. *Yale Law Journal.* Volume 43, No. 4, pp. 537–570.

For in the criminal scenario where the wife kills the husband, the female's actions are perceived as voluntary, calculated, and logical. Whereas, in the criminal scenario where the husband kills the wife, the male's actions are perceived as involuntary, kindled by unbridled passion, inability to control emotions, and uncontainable rage. How peculiar, that the common law fails to recognise the inherently natural and systematic distinction between the male and female sex, in relation to the anatomy and physiology of the human body between the two sexes.

In the English common law system that is operable within select British Commonwealth sovereign nation-states, for the wife having effectuated the murder of her husband, she is likely to receive the term of life imprisonment for her actions. Whereas, in the alternative case in which the husband murders the wife, he is likely to only receive ca. 10 to 15 years imprisonment. Both parties committed the same horrendous act. However, the female sex committed the alleged crime in such a manner that accounts for, factors into consideration, is reflective of, her physiological limitations against the male's presumed transcendental masculinity and physiological advantage over the female sex, however, the female sex is more likely than not, to receive a far harsher punishment for her crime, than the male sex defendant, at a criminal trial, if convicted and found guilty by the jury.

Notwithstanding, in both the aforementioned cases, the criminal offence is the same, a spouse has been murdered. Yet there exists, apparently in operation, a sex-based distinction, based on the manner in which the alleged criminal act is perceived to have been executed, for the common law does not appear to factor into consideration, that by the very natural distinctions between the male and the female sex, in order to secure the effectuation of an immoral and illegal criminal deed, the male and female sex would both proceed to do so by very different means. However, the terminal result of this immoral and unlawful act is identical in both cases (i.e., the murder of a spouse), whether it be the female sex or the male sex that commits this atrocious crime. Regardless of the instruments and means employed, both the male sex and the female sex committed an *actus reus* (guilty act), and both equally possess a *mens rea* (guilty mind). Therefore, the philosophical question must be posited; Is the deliverance of natural justice sexist at common law?

As a contemporary example, consider, a recent criminal law case in the matter of *D.P.P. v Ristevski (2019)* heard in the Supreme Court of Victoria, Australia, for the 2016 murder of Mrs. Karen Ristevski; the wife of Mr. Borce Ristevski, who was allegedly murdered by her husband.[900] Specifically, this contemporary legal case, where the husband is found guilty by a court of law for the murder of his wife, appears to confirm the sex inequity factor in criminal sentencing. This Australian legal case demonstrates the aforementioned gender discrimination concern, disposed favourably towards the position of the male sex, when it comes to the nation-state levying the criminal charge of murder by a husband of his wife within the domain of criminal law, as part of the broader common law legal system in force within the English common law sovereign and independent nation-states.

In his determination, the Honourable Justice Christopher William Beale, sentenced the accused, Mr. Borce Ristevski, upon being found guilty, to a 'total effective sentence of nine years' imprisonment—with a non-parole period of six years'.[901] Mr. Ristevski was initially charged with murder, but he later pleaded 'guilty' to the lesser criminal offence of manslaughter. Thereby, attracting a lenient criminal sentence than what would have otherwise been imposed upon the convicted defendant. This is confirmed and evidenced in the Honourable Justice Beale's sentencing remarks, 'Pursuant to Section 6AAA of *the Sentencing Act 1991*, I declare that, but for your plea of guilty, I would have imposed a sentence of 10 years' imprisonment with a non-parole period of seven years'.[902] Given

---

900 Director of Public Prosecutions v Ristevski [2019] VSC 253 (Beale J).
901 Justice Christopher Beale's sentencing remarks in S C.R. 2018 0213.
902 Justice Christopher Beale's sentencing remarks in S C.R. 2018 0213, p. 14.

Justice Beale's judgement in this criminal case, Mr. Ristevski could potentially be out of prison within six years for the murder of his wife in 2016. *Aequalitatem coram lege* (equality before the law) does not exist between the sexes in the contemporary modern civilised society.

996

The contemporary modern popular history has incorrectly and overly attributed the incidence of 'concentration camps' utilised by the totalitarian NAZI party during the German *Third Reich* (1933–1945) as a German innovation. In fact, concentration camps were a creation, an invention, of the British civilisation in *The Second Boer War* (1899–1902), a lesser proliferated fact of the modern history. The British civilisation ought to rightly be accredited with the original patent of this immoral invention in the modern civilised world. The British civilisation created the inhumane institution of concentration camps that fundamentally serve to deprive the modern human of dignity, life, liberty, autonomy, agency, and freedom.

Since the British civilisation's invention of concentration camps, Hitler, Lenin, Stalin, Mao, and Kim Jong-un have only replicated this inhumane, uncivilised, and barbaric institution of the British civilisation, to serve their expedient political ends within their totalitarian sovereign nation-states. It is fascinating how the modern political history is recorded, based on who documents it, and such an artificial body politic's or natural person's reputation and/or pre-eminent position in the international affairs.

Most commonly, the concentration camps are associated and accredited to the slaughter of the Jewish people by the *Führer* Adolf Hitler during the German Third *Reich* (1933–1945). This thesis does not refute this historical fact, rather it affirms to question the manner in which sovereign nation-states, international institutions, and non-governmental organisations, universities, inter-governmental organisations, the global civil society, and the human civilisation writ large, prospectively, after the established historical reality, come to partially and subjectively document, record, and disseminate the constructed conventional history of the human civilisation.

997

The Indigenous civilisations of the Commonwealth of Australia, the Dominion of Canada, New Zealand, and the United States of America have become the most marginalised and dependent people in the contemporary modern civilised world. This, in fact, is a direct consequence of the externalities of *The Great British Empire* (1670–1997); an empire that was characterised by imperialism, mercantilism, conquest, oppression, proslavery, colonialism, exploitation, world domination, and not to mention, the genocide of the Indigenous peoples and the permanent English settlement of the native lands of the Indigenous civilisations of the four newfound Bible Commonwealth Countries: the Commonwealth of Australia, the Dominion of Canada, New Zealand, and the United States of America.

During the reign of the Great British Empire, and the other Great European Powers (i.e., Belgium, Denmark, France, Germany, Italy, the Netherlands, Portugal, Spain, and Sweden), the pinnacle of the Western civilisation's colonial rule across the African, Asian, and Middle Eastern nation-states, came to ensure that the black and the coloured people of the modern civilised world definitely suffered from the negative externalities associated with colonisation; human slavery, economic exploitation, the extraction of valuable natural resources and minerals, mass murders, genocide, and the subjugation of their native lands.

However, the African, Arab, and Asian peoples suffering was temporary, (not to lessen its inhumane and immoral significance), in direct comparison to that of the First Nations Peoples of the Commonwealth of Australia, the Dominion of Canada, New Zealand,

and the United States of America. For the Indigenous peoples of the aforesaid sovereign nation-states, for whom the British civilisations' imperial conquest, genocidal extermination, human slavery, and the outright colonial dispossession of Indigenous sacred territory, which has wholly manifested into an irreversible and permanent newfound English reality of unlawful occupation and British settlement on Indigenous lands in the contemporary modern civilised world. The African, Arab, and Asian countries secured their independence, right to self-determination, right to self-government, recognition as equal sovereign nation-states in the International Community of civilised sovereign nation-states, however, none of these political gains were forthcoming for the Indigenous civilisations of the modern Bible Commonwealth countries.

In stark comparison, for the Indigenous civilisations, they have been subject to genocide, and now only continue to exist as a disadvantaged minority ethnic group in the modern Bible Commonwealth countries. These Indigenous people have been displaced in their own sovereign native land, with the alien and foreign British civilisation having permanently settled their countries. Consequently, the Indigenous civilisation and their ancient way of life has literally ceased to exist, but for the historical artefacts and Indigenous treasures that one will find located in the national museums in the Bible Commonwealth countries and in the United Kingdom of Great Britain and Northern Ireland.

What the Indigenous civilisations have been afforded in return is the symbolic and ceremonial titles of 'The First Nations Peoples' and 'The Traditional Owners' of the Commonwealth of Australia, the Dominion of Canada, New Zealand, and the United States of America. In addition to the belated enactment of the United Nations *Declaration on the Rights of Indigenous Peoples (2007)*; which oddly enough, however, unsurprisingly, the four Bible Commonwealth sovereign nation-states that are founded on, established upon, crimes against humanity; the immoral principles of genocide, human slavery, torture, and the near total extinction of the Indigenous civilisation, all voted against this declaration's adoption at the United Nations in New York City, namely, the Commonwealth of Australia, the Dominion of Canada, New Zealand, and the United States of America.[903]

998

On the Cold War (1947–1991) in the Third World. As the twentieth-century *Cold War* history of International Relations has demonstrated, in the event that a supreme head of state of a sovereign nation-state, is not subservient, or stands in opposition to, the U.K. and the U.S. national interests and foreign policy objectives, then that particular third-world nation-state sovereign leader will more likely than not, be removed from political power and deposed by means of a military coup.[904] A prime case study example is the 1953 political coup that toppled the Iranian Prime Minister Mohammad Mosaddegh (r. 1951–1953) from power in Iran.

In addition, also consider the first Prime Minister of an independent and sovereign Republic of Congo, Patrice Lumumba (1925–1961), who also confronted a similar ordeal in 1961. Prime Minister Lumumba, was a staunch African nationalist leader who stood for the universally applicable principles of freedom, independence, self-determination, self-government, and the end to foreign Belgian colonial rule in the Congo. All ideals of political

---

903 The United Nations Declaration on the Rights of Indigenous Peoples (UNDRIP) was adopted by the United Nations General Assembly on Thursday, 13 September 2007, by a majority of 144 nation-states in favour, with 4 votes against (i.e., Australia, Canada, New Zealand and the United States), and 11 abstentions (i.e., Azerbaijan, Bangladesh, Bhutan, Burundi, Colombia, Georgia, Kenya, Nigeria, Russian Federation, Samoa, and Ukraine). See: United Nations Department of Economic and Social Affairs. (2020). *United Nations Declaration on the Rights of Indigenous Peoples*. United Nations Department of Economic and Social Affairs. Date accessed: 24 February 2020. Access link: <https://www.un.org/development/desa/Indigenouspeoples/declaration-on-the-rights-of-Indigenous-peoples.html>

904 President, Prime Minister, King, Queen, Prince, or Princess.

governance that are consistent with *The United Nations Charter (1945)*, however, Lumumba was assassinated in a political coup with the support of the Kingdom of Belgium and the U.S. Not to mention, Lumumba was replaced with a U.S. backed dictator Mobutu Sese Seko during the superpower conflict of the *Cold War*, to be subservient and faithful to the Western Imperial power's foreign policy objectives.[905]

Notwithstanding, Prime Minister Lumumba's grand vision for an optimistic future for the Republic of Congo, his tenure as the first Prime Minister of an independent and sovereign Congo, and his life, was tragically short-lived. This is a direct and consequential attribute of the foreign Western Power's interference in the internal affairs of a sovereign Congo vis-à-vis a staged political coup in the newly independent and sovereign nation-state in 1961.

A *coup d'état* orchestrated by the Belgium, British, and the U.S. intelligence agencies and government officials to remove Prime Minister Lumumba from political power.[906, 907, 908] Why? Self-evidently, similar to the fervent nationalist and anti-imperialist leaders such as the Iranian Prime Minister Mosaddegh, Castro of Cuba, Nasser of Egypt, Nehru of India, Nkrumah of Ghana, Mao of China, Tito of Yugoslavia, Minh of Vietnam, Gaddafi of Libya, and Lenin of the Soviet Union, Lumumba stood up to defiantly assert the self-evident and unalienable political and civil rights of the Congolese people in the twentieth century. A time in the modern world history that was a period of great political turmoil and regional instability in the poor Third World, with the global

---

905 Afoaku, Osita G. (1997). The U.S. and Mobutu Sese Seko: Waiting on Disaster. *Journal of Third World Studies*. Volume 14, No. 1, (Spring, 1997), pp. 65–90.
906 France-Presse, Agence. (2002). *World Briefing I Europe: Belgium: Apology for Lumumba Killing*. New York Times Archives. Date accessed: 30 June 2019. Access link: <https://www.nytimes.com/2002/02/06/world/world-briefing-europe-belgium-apology-for-lumumba-killing.html>
907 Park, Daphne. (2013). Letters. *London Review of Books*, p. 4.
908 Stockwell, John. (1978). *In Search of Enemies: A C.I.A. Story*. New York: W.W. Norton & Company, p. 105.

CHAPTER 6 | HISTORY AND JURISPRUDENCE

Superpower ideological battle of the *Cold War* in the immediate background, and the decolonisation movement.

999

There will never be a universal peace without first a catastrophic world war, for each sovereign empire (including the political, economic, and social order) is founded upon the fundamental political objectives of decisive unilateral military victory of one of the belligerents; resulting in the unconditional surrender of the enemy, and the subjugation of the conquered and defeated people and their territory. Therefore, regardless of the contemporary institutionalised political, economic, and social order, there will always exist resistance against that oppressive order which is founded on an unjust peace. Which in turn to such resistance, shall be met with the employment of force by the occupying power against the conquered people and their nation-states.

Ultimately, there will arise a point in time where the status quo political, economic, and social order will be decimated, giving way to a new world order founded upon a novel political ideology, undergirded by force and terror, sustained by the institution of positive laws, until its destined demise is met, and so forth, *ad infinitum*. In the final analysis, there cannot exist a universal peace across the human civilisation, without the tenets of social justice, eternal law, social equality, the equal distribution of private wealth and natural resources for the greater universal benefit of humankind.

1,000

This stanza examines the ideas that gave rise to and underwrite the political organisation of the industrialised, urbanised, Westernised, privatised, globalised, secularised, colonised, liberalised, Anglicised, and modernised society, and not to mention, the negative externalities that arise as a consequence of modernity in the physical world. In addition, the latter component of this stanza proposes a fundamental solution to the organisation of the body politic that is responsible for the political and socio-economic governance of the modern civilised society.

On the modern concept of the ownership and possession of private property and personal wealth, in addition to the modern concepts of the division and specialisation of human labour. The ideas of private property, profit maximisation, private enterprise, pecuniary gains, personal wealth accumulation, and the exploitation of human labour power, all serve to create artificial distinctions of inequality across the modern human civilisation; an inequality that is material and economic in its nature. Consequently, creating a false distinction of a socio-economic class-based modern society; a hierarchical society, predominantly consisting of:

- The royal ruling class (i.e., pharaoh, emperor, heavenly sovereign, tsar, king, queen, grand duke, earl, supreme leader, caliph, and grand prince).
- The political elite ruling class (i.e., president, vice-president, prime minister, senator, speaker of the house, chief justice of the supreme court, and attorney-general).
- The economic elite class as guided by the established medical and legal professions (i.e., lawyers, barristers, solicitors, magistrates, justices, chief justice, surgeon, anaesthesiologist, medical doctor, and medical specialists).
- The poor-working class (i.e., unskilled labourers, factory workers, cleaners, office workers, and construction site workers).
- The welfare class (i.e., homeless, disabled, disadvantaged segments of the population, and incapacitated individuals).

The inequity of the constituents within each socio-economic class in the industrialised, urbanised, globalised, privatised, and modernised civilised society is distinguished by the factors of noble or common rank at birth, the economic value of one's human labour power, and the monetary value of one's personal wealth and private assets. In the absence of artificial concepts such as private property, personal wealth, private enterprise, royalty, nobility, socio-economic class divisions of the conventional society, and the division and specialisation of human labour, naturalism; the natural state of human affairs within the human society would prevail, and render a classless conventional society, provisioning the true state of universal equality of the human civilisation.

In addition, the presence of material and socio-economic distinctions in the human society artificially creates relative poverty, social class distinctions, and socio-economic inequality, rather than fostering dynamism, and ensures the unjust oppression of the poor and unlettered working-class majority constituents within the modern conventional society. For the financial capital domination, social class oppression, and economic exploitation of the poor masses by the aristocratic class; the royalty, the nobility, the gentry, the extravagantly wealthy politically influential constituents, and the constituents of the established medical and legal professional class is omnipresent in the modern civilised society.

The aristocracy, artificially and collectively, function to create the societal context to ensure the legal, economic, social, and political subjugation and oppression of the unlettered common masses; the members of the poor working-class and welfare class of the modern industrialised conventional society.[909, 910] William Shakespeare's play *Coriolanus* demonstrates the amoral sentiment

---

909 'The people of England regards itself as free; but it is grossly mistaken; it is free only during the election of members of parliament. As soon as they are elected, slavery overtakes it, and it is nothing.' See: Rousseau, Jean Jacques. (Victor Gourevitch, Ed.) (1997). *Rousseau: 'The Social Contract' and Other Later Political Writings*. Cambridge: Cambridge University Press, p. 114.
910 In the United Kingdom of Great Britain and Northern Ireland consider:
The Statute of Cambridge 1388
The Vagabonds Act 1572
The Act for the Relief of the Poor 1597
The Act for the Relief of the Poor 1601
The Poor Law Amendment Act 1834

of modern politicians, and how it is based on the naked exploitation of the mass populace of a sovereign and independent nation-state:

> *'The Senators of Rome are this good belly, and you the mutinous members, for examine their counsels and their cares, digest things rightly touching the weal o' the common, you shall find no public benefit that you receive, but it proceeds or comes from them to you, and no way from yourselves.'*[911]

Competing theological, economic, religious, political, social, and secular ideologies (i.e., Catholicism, Maoism, Socialism, Liberalism, Communism, Fascism, Capitalism, Marxism, Neoliberalism, Globalism, Trotskyism, Nationalism, Republicanism, Leninism, and Feminism), do not terminally resolve the inherent political, social, and economic inequality present within an ordered civil society of a sovereign and independent nation-state. In fact, they merely represent an alternative novel fundamental ideology to govern the poor working-class masses and direct the trajectory of the extraction of the unlettered masses' productive human labour power surplus, for the benefit of the minority of aristocratic constituents of the modern conventional society, who entertain positions of royal authority and/ or the exercise of political power; a power that ultimately vests in the collective sovereign people of a modern independent nation-state.

The terminal solution resides in the abolition of abstract and intellectual ideologies, and the nationalisation of economic and financial industries that destroy the artificial societal structures that promote oligarchy and nepotism within the bureaucratic private and public institutions of a sovereign nation-state. The end political objective herein is to eliminate all perceived socio-economic inequity and human-made poverty amongst constituents within the modern civilised society.

---

911   Shakespeare, William. (1608). *Coriolanus*. Act 1, Scene 1.

Furthermore, this essay proposes the effectuation of a transfer of political and legal power within a nation-state into a 'Sovereign Governing Council' of several constituents and organs, whom are best equipped to promote the greater good, the 'public interest' of the majority poor working-class masses, which is the final objective of the just and equitable human society.[912] As opposed to an affluent minority of the exalted and opulent aristocratic class who most unjustly exploit their privileged positions of high public office, in order to further advance their own self-interests and egotistical agendas within the confines of an independent body politic.

In order to ensure that the appointed citizens of the sovereign nation-state, the legitimate representatives of the people, are of fit and proper character to take lawful admission and the sacred oath of high public office into the 'Sovereign Governing Council', such public servants are themselves to be strictly regulated to serve the utilitarian philosophical ends of the maximisation of the greater public good of all constituents of the body politic. To the furtherance of this just, moral, and most noble endeavour, the political constituents ought to satisfy the stringent prerequisites and article requirements to effectuate political rule and governance within the sovereign nation-state as prescribed by the *Charter of the Sovereign Governing Council*. For the sake of clarity, in all public affairs concerning political rule and governance within the body politic, no deviation, under any circumstances whatsoever, is permitted from the aforesaid Charter.

---

912   Lodge, Rupert Clendon. (1927). The Platonic Highest Good (I). *The Philosophical Review*. Volume 36, No. 5, (September, 1927), pp. 428–449.
Demos, Raphael. (1937). Plato's Idea of the Good. *The Philsophical Review*. Volume 46, No. 3, (May, 1937), pp. 245–275.

THE CHARTER OF THE SOVEREIGN GOVERNING COUNCIL

Eligibility

Article I

Antecedent to the consideration of a citizen of the sovereign nation-state to be eligible for a position within the Sovereign Governing Council ('the Council'), such a citizen must not possess pre-existing children, be they biological, or adopted.

Article II

The citizen, of male or female sex, must voluntarily consent to a medical and surgical procedure of sterilisation, in order to ensure that such a natural person is rendered incapacitated of the future capacity to conceive. That is to infer, the biological function of human sexual reproduction is to be terminated, and the real possibility of conceiving future offspring for the constituent is to be wholly severed and rendered inoperable.

Article III

Any citizen of the sovereign nation-state, but for those citizens who have previously served on the Council, that satisfy the requirements of Article I and II of the Charter of the Sovereign Governing Council ('the Charter'), may furnish an application for consideration of the Executive Committee for the Management and Governance of the Council ('the Committee'), for admission as an Honourable Fellow to the Council.

Appointment

Article IV

Upon a citizen's appointment to the Council, that citizen is to be conferred with the title of 'Honourable Fellow' of the Council.

Article V

A maximum and a fixed governance term limit of twenty (20) years of continuous service applies to all Honourable Fellows elected to the Council. This 20-year term limit is to be effective and calculated from the date that the citizen is appointed to the rank of Honourable Fellow and admitted to the Council in accordance with *Article IV* of the Charter.

Governance of Fellows'

Article VI

An Honourable Fellow of the Council, who is elected by the Committee, is to have one's personal affairs directly managed by the Trustee for the Fellows of the Sovereign Governing Council ('the Trustee'). Under no circumstances is an Honourable Fellow of the Council authorised to manage one's personal affairs.

Article VII

The Trustee is to have its own governing Charter and by-laws, that affirm who may or may not be appointed as an agent for the Trustee. The Trustee has fiduciary duties to all Honourable Fellows and must be an independent entity, to the maximum extent permissible by law, and none of its agents shall have served on the Council, or be affiliated, politically or otherwise, with any other related organ of the Council's apparatus. In addition, the agents of the Trustee are not to have family, kinship, or blood relations to the Honourable Fellows of the Council. The agents of the Trustee are to have fixed terms of ten (10) years of continuous service.

Article VIII

The appointment and cessation of Honourable Fellows to the Council is to be governed by the Executive Committee for the Management and Governance of the Council ('the Committee').

Article IX
The Committee is to have its own governing charter and by-laws, that affirm who may or may not be appointed as an agent to the Committee. The Committee has fiduciary duties to the Council, and must be an independent entity, to the maximum extent permissible by law, and none of its agents shall have served on the Council or the Trustee entity, or any other affiliated organ of the Council's apparatus. The Committee's agents are not to have any family, blood, or kinship relations to the Honourable Fellows of the Council. The agents of the Committee are to have fixed terms of ten (10) years of continuous service.

Regulations and by-laws of the Sovereign Governing Council

Article X
The Council is to have a total membership of eleven (11) members at any given point in time. This total membership is to be comprised of ten (10) Honourable Fellows at all times, with the minimum and an equal number of five (5) male and female Honourable Fellows at any given point in time. In addition, the Council is to have one (1) President at all times.

Article XI
All of the Council's resolutions are binding and have the force of law in the territory of the sovereign nation-state. The resolutions are to pass by a formal vote by the Honourable Fellows of the Council, with a majority in number (6 or more Honourable Fellows voting in favour of the proposed resolution). All the casted votes are to constitute a 'Yes' or 'No' determination to proposed resolutions, no abstentions are permitted on a vote concerning a matter of law.

Article XII
In the event that a proposed resolution does not carry on the casted votes, it may be further debated at the next-sitting session of the Council, and amended as appropriate for a future vote. In the event that a proposed resolution does carry on the casted votes, it is to

CHAPTER 6 | HISTORY AND JURISPRUDENCE

receive presidential assent within ten (10) days, and upon such presidential assent it becomes law within the sovereign body politic, and as such embodies the force of law.

Article XIII
The Honourable Fellows are to meet at least two (2) times a week for general hearing sessions of the Council that further the development of the sovereign nation-state and the betterment of its citizens. The particulars of convening such hearing sessions shall be made in accordance with the reasonable convenience of the majority of the Honourable Fellows of the Council.

Article XIV
The Honourable Fellows may convene for a special session of the Council at any time to attend to a national crisis. A special session may be called at the discretion of the President or any Honourable Fellow of the Council, with at least six (6) hours' notice prior to such a special session's intended date and time. The particulars of convening such a special session shall be made in accordance with the convenience of the majority of the Honourable Fellows of the Council.

For the express purposes of the lawful exercise of this article, a 'national crisis' is explicitly defined as; a crisis that represents a grave danger to the welfare of the citizens of the sovereign nation-state, however, a national crisis does not extend beyond the territorial demarcations and jurisdiction of the sovereign nation-state, and it does not represent an existential threat to the sovereign nation-state. Under no circumstances whatsoever does the occurrence of unarmed civilian protests in the sovereign nation-state constitute a national crisis.

Article XV
The President may convene an emergency session of the Council during a time or an event that presents an imminent and grave threat to the national security of the sovereign nation-state. To convene an

emergency session of the Council, no notice is required, and it shall be convened as soon as practicable for the Honourable Fellows and President to arrange such an extraordinary meeting of the Council.

For the express purposes of the lawful exercise of this article, a threat to 'national security' is explicitly defined as; an immediate existential threat to the continuation, or existence of the sovereign nation-state, a declaration or condition of actual war to which the sovereign nation-state is a belligerent party, the welfare of the majority of the citizens of the sovereign nation-state is in grave danger, there is, or is imminent, the onset of a natural or human-made disaster (i.e., cyclone, flash flood, famine, bushfire, epidemic, terrorist attack, pandemic, or a severe economic recession), or a violent political revolution is underway that employs lethal force and is symbolic of an orchestrated political coup that is supported by hostile foreign forces, and is designed to undermine and overthrow the Sovereign Governing Council, as the legitimate people's assembly of the sovereign nation-state.

Only the President may exercise discretion and give Presidential direction to the Council to convene an emergency session of the Sovereign Governing Council. Under no circumstances whatsoever does the occurrence of unarmed civilian protests constitute a national security threat.

Article XVI
During times of national security threats or an internal crisis, the President is not authorised to initiate emergency powers or 'rule by decree'. At all times political determinations are to be effectuated by the consensus of the Honourable Fellows, and the democratic political decision-making process vests exclusively in the Council. The Council is alone the 'sovereign' body, however, the President, as a natural person, is considered *primus inter pares* (first among equals) of the eleven constituents of the Sovereign Governing Council.

CHAPTER 6 | HISTORY AND JURISPRUDENCE

Article XVII

The sovereign nation-state is to consist of eight ministries that are each tasked with legal responsibility for a distinct area of public governance of the sovereign nation-state (see *Article XVIII*). The head of each of the eight ministries is to report directly to the Council on a half-yearly and yearly basis, and provide the Council with progress reports and substantial updates as to the execution and implementation of the Council's resolutions, directives, and agendas for the further economic development, national prosperity, and political governance of the sovereign nation-state.

In addition, a three-hour convocation session is to be held on a half-yearly and yearly basis that is to be personally attended by the head of the ministry, and all the Honourable Fellows and the President of the Council. The minutes of such sessions are to be made publicly available for the perusal of all citizens of the sovereign nation-state. All meetings between the ministries and the Council are open sessions to the public, and therefore, may be attended by the citizens of the sovereign nation-state, this function serves the express purpose of maintaining an informed, educated, and knowledgeable citizenry of the sovereign nation-state on matters concerning public governance of the body politic.

Functions of the Executive Committee for the Management and Governance of the Council and its associated ministries

Article XVIII

The Committee is to nominate the head of the eight state ministries, the nominations for the position of the head of the ministry is subject to the final endorsement of the Council. Such ministries are established to regulate a select component of public affairs of the citizens of the sovereign nation-state for the utmost public interest and greater good of the people. The public servants of the various ministries of the sovereign nation-state shall be selected for appointment on the basis of equal opportunity and with utmost regard to the principle of meritocracy.

All citizens of the sovereign nation-state possess the inalienable political right and the irrevocable legal right to make a written application to apply for a position of public service at any of the eight ministries of the nation-state, to that specific ministry directly. But for the position of the Head of Ministry, which is to be exclusively administered for selection by the Executive Committee for the Management and Governance of the Council and the Council's endorsement. Furthermore, all citizens of the sovereign nation-state possess the political and legal right to make an application for the Head of a Ministry, however, must address that written application directly to the aforementioned Committee. The nation-state's eight ministries include:

- Ministry of Internal Security, Law, and Justice
- Ministry of Foreign Affairs and International Commerce
- Ministry of National Defence
- Ministry of Treasury, Economics, and Finance
- Ministry of Education
- Ministry of Health
- Ministry of Transport
- Ministry of Citizen's Welfare

Presidency of the Sovereign Governing Council

Article XIX
The Committee, as a collective whole, is to determine who will be appointed as the founding and successive President of the Council. The President must be selected from one of the existing ten (10) Honourable Fellows of the Council. No citizen of the sovereign nation-state shall be directly considered for the position of President, but must have previously served as an Honourable Fellow of the Council.

Article XX
The President of the Council shall serve a single fixed term of no more than five (5) years of continuous service. After which period

of time the President may determine to retire, or return as a 'Honourable Fellow' to the Council, subject to the operable time limitation of service to the Council as defined in *Article V*; which stipulates that no Honourable Fellow may remain as an elected constituent to the Council for a period of time exceeding that of twenty (20) years of service. Failing the exercise, or applicability, of a return of the President to the position of Honourable Fellow to the Council, the President must then proceed to immediately resign from the Council.

Article XXI
In the event that an Honourable Fellow has been appointed for more than fifteen (15) years of continuous service within the Sovereign Governing Council, that Honourable Fellow shall not be considered as an eligible candidate for the position of President of the Council.

Article XXII
The President may exercise a casting vote in the event that there exists a deadlock (5–5) voting outcome on the passage of a proposed resolution, draft legislation, bill, or an agenda item tabled for the Council's consideration. In the event of a voting deadlock, the President's exercise of the casting vote determination, 'For' or 'Against', is final and binding on the proposed resolution, draft legislation, bill, or an agenda item vote and its outcome.

Citizens' rights

Article XXII
Any citizen of the sovereign nation-state can propose a case for the enactment of new legislation, the amendment of existing legislation, or the repeal of existing legislation. In addition, any citizen may raise any agenda matter deemed appropriate for the Council's consideration. This process of direct political action and proactive stakeholder intervention ensures that each and every citizen has a meaningful voice in the political process and public governance of the sovereign nation-state.

Article XXIII
The Bureau of Citizen's Political Advocacy ('the Bureau') is entrusted with the responsibility to carefully consider all applications by citizens of the sovereign nation-state and determine whether or not to propose a matter raised by a citizen, as an agenda item for the Council's consideration.

Article XXIV
The Bureau is to have its own governing charter and by-laws, that affirm who may or may not be appointed as an agent to the Bureau. The Bureau must be an independent entity, to the maximum extent permissible by law, and none of its agents shall have served on the Committee, the Council, the Trustee, or any other affiliated organ of the Council's apparatus. The Bureau's agents are not to have any family, blood, or kinship relations to the Honourable Fellows of the Council. The members of the Bureau are to have fixed terms of ten (10) years of continuous service.

Article XXV
In the event that the Bureau determines not to endorse a citizen's proposal for the consideration of the Council, it must confirm this negative determination in writing to the citizen within sixty (60) business days of the citizen first raising the case with the Bureau. In the event that the citizen remains dissatisfied with the determination and the reasons for the Bureau's determination, the citizen retains the legal right, which crystallises at this point in time, as a redress, to then write and express one's case directly to the President of the Council.

The President of the Council has the vested powers to exercise presidential discretion and to override the Bureau, to have a citizen's particular case incorporated into the agenda for the Council's consideration at its next general session. However, the President can only exercise political power to positively affirm citizen's cases, upon appeal, that, in the first instance, had been rejected by the Bureau for the Council's deliberation. The President shall not exercise this vested authority in the negative sense; namely, to veto cases that have already been affirmed by the Bureau to form part of the agenda of the Council at its next general session.

Oversight of the Sovereign Governing Council

Article XXVI

The Sovereign Governing Council Regulatory and Compliance Board ('the Board') is to investigate all complaints against any ministry, head of ministry, employee of ministry, or state institution of the body politic. This includes complaints against the Honourable Fellows and the President of the Council.

Article XXVII

The Board is to have its own governing charter and by-laws, that affirm who may or may not be appointed as an agent to the Board. The Board must at all times be perceived and actually be, an independent entity, to the maximum extent permissible by law, and none of its agents shall have served on the Council, the Trustee, the Bureau, the Committee, the Authority, or any other affiliated organ of the Council's apparatus. The Board's agents are not to have any family, blood, or kinship relations to the Honourable Fellows or the President of the Council. The members of the Board are to have fixed terms of ten (10) years of continuous service.

Article XXVIII

The Board possesses the investigative powers to suspend, re-designate, or dismiss any member from any ministry or state institution of the sovereign nation-state, shall it find admissible evidence and categorical proof that such a member has engaged in fraud, criminal activity, an attempt to undermine the territorial integrity of the sovereign nation-state, or serious political misconduct, subject to a proper and thorough investigation in accordance with the equitable principles of: the rule of law, procedural fairness, natural justice, and with proper regard to due process. However, the Honourable Fellows or the President of the Council can only be removed with the co-operation and mutual consent of the Committee. The President does not possess presidential privilege or legal immunity by virtue of the exclusive position held within the Council.

Article XXIX
All monetary and financial affairs of the Council, its departments, organs, and ministries are to be managed and endorsed by the Monetary Financial Authority of the Sovereign Governing Council ('the Authority').

Article XXX
The Authority is to have its own governing charter and by-laws, that affirm who may or may not be appointed as an agent to the Authority. The Authority must at all times be perceived and actually be, an independent entity, to the maximum extent permissible by law, and none of its agents shall have served on the Council, the Trustee entity, the Committee, the Board, or any other affiliated organ of the Council's apparatus. The Authority's agents are not to have any family, blood, or kinship relations to the Honourable Fellows or the President of the Council. The members of the Authority are to have fixed terms of ten (10) years of continuous service.

Auxiliary content

- In so far as it is practically possible, the Charter serves to ensure the political constituents of the Council are free from the pursuit of self-interested desires, egotistical motives, pecuniary gain, nepotism, power struggles, hidden agendas, personal aims, and private objectives.
- The Charter aims to further ensure that the political organisation of the sovereign nation-state is solely for the express purpose to maximise the public interest, and no Honourable Fellow or President of the Council takes advantage of the high position in public office, to exercise functions and duties

vested in that particular position for an improper, illegal, or unconstitutional purpose.
- The Honourable Fellows and the President of the Council are to be exclusively dedicated to the transcendental pursuit of the public interest; the greater good of the civil society within the sovereign nation-state. Thus, for the political constituents, there cannot exist the presence of causal factors that create the grounds for the concurrent and co-existence of private interest and public interest in the body politic.
- The very notion of the fundamental compatibility of private interest and public interest are antithetical. The furtherance of self-interest and the public interest are two mutually exclusive endeavours; they cannot co-exist in parallel, and therefore, remain irreconcilable. There can be no synthesis of the public-interest and the self-interest, without the furtherance of one of them, being to the direct or perceived detriment of the other.
- The Charter aims to eliminate the undesirable situation whereby conflict of interest arises in the political governance of the sovereign nation-state, both *perceived* and *actual* conflict of interest. In addition, the Charter aspires to transcend the known base limitations of human nature, and thereby, create the requisite conditions to ensure political authority is not exercised for personal gain or the pursuit of self-interest, by those political leaders in whom such political authority is vested, but rather ensure that such political authority is exercised objectively and impartially to the highest degree, for the proper and express purpose of the betterment and development of the sovereign nation-state and its people's welfare.

This is a four volume treatise on philosophy.
This is the end of Volume III of IV.
The treatise is continued in Volume IV of IV.

www.ingramcontent.com/pod-product-compliance
Lightning Source LLC
Chambersburg PA
CBHW061405160426
42811CB00114B/2383/J